365 SOUPS

by Bon Viveur

Bon Viveur is the pen-name of Johnnie and Fanny
Cradock, the famous husband and wife team of
gourmets and cooks. In *The Daily Telegraph*, where
they write regularly on cookery, on television, and on
stage all over the country, the Cradocks have taught
many thousands of women—and men and children—
how to cook and to enjoy doing it.

a 𝔇𝔞𝔦𝔩𝔶 𝔗𝔢𝔩𝔢𝔤𝔯𝔞𝔭𝔥 book of recipes

First issued 1977
Reprinted 1982
© Daily Telegraph and author

The Daily Telegraph,
135 Fleet Street, London EC4P 4BL
Printed in Great Britain by
Richard Clay (The Chaucer Press) Ltd,
Bungay, Suffolk

Contents

INTRODUCTION

The legend has grown very strong in recent years that stock pots are time-consuming to prepare, skim and maintain. Our first duty therefore is to disabuse your minds of this fallacy by explaining just how easily the job may be done even if you happen to be a career woman as well as a home-maker. In this circumstance we assume you will be away from home for fairly lengthy periods during the day. So let us go straight to the heart of the matter and list the facts which enable any woman to have a good supply of modest stocks on which she can draw for a vast number of filling, nourishing soups with which to take the sharp edge off family appetites before the costly main course makes its appearance at table.

Cooking
1. **Stocks of any kind can be as easily made in the oven in sturdy casseroles as in stockpots on top burners.**
2. Stockpots can be maintained for 7 to 10 days at least, **if** the contents are raised to boiling point and then simmered for 20 minutes daily.

Skimming
3. The skimming of fat from the top of a newly completed pot of stock can be done instantly, as explained later on. There is no need to wait until the liquor is cold, and the fat forms a thick crust on the top which can then be cut away.

If you put raw meat, game or pultry bones and game and poultry carcases into a casserole, cover liberally with cold water, cover casserole and put on the floor of the oven (a.m. or p.m.) at 240 F (Gas $\frac{1}{4}$). You can leave the stock undisturbed, either until you come down the next morning or until you return home in the evening. You will find that you have an admirable brew of stock waiting for you, ready to strain and use.

If your stock is not sufficiently strongly flavoured for any particular requirement (indicated in our recipes by the phrase "strongly-reduced stock") you merely measure off **twice** the quantity indicated in the recipe and simmer down steadily until this has reduced itself to the given quantity.

If you require the most concentrated of all forms of stock, called "glaze", which is the name applied to a thick syrupy mixture which makes a shiny and very flavoursome coating, you merely simmer on until you achieve just this. You can expect to obtain about 3 to 4 fluid oz from a quart of stock.

If you wish to use stock immediately and can see as you take the pot from the oven that the top is covered with liquid fat, remove this quickly and easily by towing a few sheets of absorbent kitchen paper or tissue paper over the surface.

When it comes to the daily re-boiling and simmering, if you put your pot on when you put on the first kettle, it will be bubbling by the time you are dressed. Then the 20 minutes simmering can be done over breakfast and the heat then turned off. Thus you leave the stock ready to skim in the old, classic way, when you return in the afternoon or evening.

Certainly we think you will agree that this clears the way to the easy making of everyday stock; but it does still leave an area for waste and disaster which we must clear up before going any further.

For if you want your stock pot to be rendered quite useless and reduced to a bubbling, fermenting mess, just put in any of the root vegetables, like potatoes, turnips, parsnips, carrots etc.

But all members of the onion family are safe; parsley roots, well washed and scraped are super because they and the parsley stalks contain all the flavour of this herb—the heads are purely decorative.

Of course you can use root vegetables sometimes. Indeed you can make wholly "vegetable" stocks but the life of these is very brief and runs something like this . . . make one day, use for soup second day, boil up remainder, simmer gently for 20 minutes and use up completely on the third day. Even so that third day is questionable in very hot weather.

One autumn, in the Daily Telegraph we published four of our own gleanings-from-the-kitchen-garden Vegetable Soups, which were immensely popular. They come into the category of almost-a-meal-in-itself soups, strictly for family occasions and quite unsuitable for the first course at a small dinner party. All four call for either meat bone or mixed vegetable stock.

If you wish to particularise for family meals then you have a wide range from which to choose. On meat alone, and, nowadays, without recourse to what our mothers and grand-mothers called "soup meat", which has priced itself out of our homes, you have pork, beef, veal, lamb, mutton and bacon bones from which to make your selection, veal being the only one which truly comes under the category of White Stock. Of these, veal is undoubtedly the most costly whilst bacon bones (for which our butcher makes no charge) are clearly the cheapest. We find that a mixture of pork bones and bacon bones, in the proportions 3 pork to 1 bacon (because of the saltiness of the latter) covered liberally with cold water, brought to the boil, then simmered for at least 4 hours makes an excellent basic brew. Remember too that unsalted pig trotters are an ideal addition, particularly if you want your stock to "jell".

Then there are poultry and game bones to be considered. Here we do urge you most strongly to smash down any such carcase to as near pulp as possible as there is juice and flavour in those bones. Thus you are only doing, with anything from an old flat-iron to a classic meat-batter, what is done on the very highest level with a game press. This supremely costly item works like an old fashioned wine press, and is used—for just one example—in the making of *Caneton Sauvage à la Presse*. The par-roasted bird, breast slices removed, is put into the press and the top bar turned and turned. Gradually as you turn, so the press forces out the rich juices thereby pro-ducing the basis for the sauce in this very famous dish.

Say you have removed the leg and thigh bones from a small turkey to turn into a Family Turkey Pie. You have then decided to use the two plump breasts to make the main course at a dinner party. The wish-bone, oysters, liver and *ailerons* (wing-tips) have been reserved for a dish of Devilled Turkey and Rice thus leaving you with the raw carcase and skin. Smash this down ruthlessly. Put it into your chosen pot, give it an onion, with or without a few cloves stuck into it—sink in a faggot of herbs comprising a strip of dried orange peel (dry on floor of oven when in use), I fat sprig of thyme, 3 peppercorns, 1 torn bay leaf, 3 sturdy parsley stalks, cover with cold water, bring to the boil, skim thoroughly so as to remove all that nasty scum which rises to the top. Throw in a further tumblerful of cold water and cook on floor of oven as already explained.

When it comes to fish stocks we must quote Escoffier for no one has ever recorded wiser culinary advice and, moreover, advice which is as topical today as when his masterpieces were written.

White Fish Stock

1 lb trimmings and bones
2 of sole or whiting,
* oz thinly-sliced, blanched*
* onions,*

2 stout parsley stalks,
⅛ bottle of white wine,
juice of a lemon,
1 quart cold water.

Butter the bottom of a thick stewpan, put in the blanched onions and the parsley stalks and upon these aromatics lay the fish remains. Add the (strained) juice of one lemon, cover the pan and allow the fish to exude its essence, jerking the pan meanwhile (1 minute). Moisten first with the wine and with the lid off, reduce to half by rapid bubbling. Add the 1 quart of cold water, bring to the boil, skim and then leave to cook for 20 minutes only on a moderate heat.

Escoffier adds, "The time allowed is ample for the purpose of extracting the aromatic and gelatinous properties contained in the bones and a more protracted stewing would only impair the flavour of the stock." There is a further note in which Escoffier stresses the importance of using minimal liquids, cooking fast and avoiding the reduction otherwise made necessary as, he emphasises "fish stock may be greatly improved by rapid cooking so as to avoid prolonged reduction." This type of stock is made and used straightaway. At the most, it may be strained, chilled, covered and refrigerated overnight for use on the following morning.

The Family Stockpot

We have no compunction in adding to our stockpot as the week progresses. If we are chining and dividing a best end neck into cutlets, in goes the chine bone and any cutlet trimmings. If we are boning out a brisket for rolling and salting, those bones go in too and should a chicken carcase eventualise we add it to the rest. It is a counsel of perfection to segregate the various meats and poultry but we do have Escoffier's authority for not doing so.

As you may have guessed by this time we adore soups and can never get enough of them. "When in doubt make a Family Brew", is our cry and so the compilation of this book is a genuine labour of love, although there is a certain element of hate in so doing at the present time when absolutely no classical meat and poultry additions may be made to our stock pots thanks to the current prices.

Before we finish with stockpots we would like to add one more very modern but highly practical justification for keeping one, at least, in your home. Not only can you make excellent soups from them but you can also turn a tin of soup into something delicious if you make your dilutions with well-reduced stock.

Not only is this true of the standard types of tinned soups but also of the more costly, rather special ones. If the contents of a tin of Lobster Bisque is stirred into one pint of Escoffier's Fish Stock (page 7) and then given a little cream, you can look smug and leave folk to draw their own conclusions as to whether you actually made the whole thing or not.

If you have cause to use shrimps or prawns for some dish, then reserve the heads, tails and shells for **Shrimp Velouté** made by adding plentifully to Escoffier Fish Stock, after the first 5 minutes of simmering, and produce really acceptable soup with only a ladleful or two or **Soup Velouté** (page 19) and a spoonful of cream added. Strain the stock first of course, then stir in the additions plus some black pepper and if you can float a shrimp or two on top of each bowlful, then so much the better. This suggestion will serve to illustrate the way in which we reserve shells of everything from cockles to lobster to use to give us yet another warming and welcome soup.

Soups
These fall into distinct categories. We reasoned that if we put all of one category together you would then be able to narrow down your arc of choice and not wade through recipes which would prove useless to you on any particular day. For example you would look under **Veloutés** if you had no stock or under

Vegetable Soups if you had only vegetable stock and so on. . . .

The classic groupings are **Veloutés, Crèmes, Purées, Potages, Consommés, Bouillons** and **Bisques**. Concerning fish soups, there are also many with quite different names like Matelots, Cotriades, Bouillabaisse and the Bisques which only relate to shellfish of one kind or another. The range of Bisques is probably the most limited, even as the range of variants on the Consommé theme are almost limitless. Indeed this category divides itself into **Consommés en Gelée** and **Consommés Chauds**. Each province of France which has a seaboard likewise has its fish soup speciality and some of the best are to be found in the North. The most over-rated, the most indigestible, and generally uncomfortable of them all is Bouillabaisse an assembly of 14 different Mediterranean fish which are not obtainable in cooler waters, will in no case be authentic when made elsewhere and. so this particular meal-and-more-in-itself will NOT find its way onto these pages.

There is also another category, **Meal-In-Themselves-Soups**, which require eating as well as drinking, and which totally preclude the participant from more than a nibble of cheese and a mouthful of fruit thereafter. Even the most passionate gourmands among the French themselves will concur upon this point!

Points to remember

Unless otherwise specified "eggs" indicates standard size throughout; "flour" automatically implies self-raising flour; "oil", pure olive oil; "vinegar", wine vinegar; "salt", either French *gros sel* or English sea salt; "pepper" means freshly milled black peppercorns, unless otherwise specified; "milk" for soups means the best you can possibly manage. All references to "pork fat" means raw, unsalted pork fat on the rind, obtainable from any pork butcher.

"Worcestershire Sauce" implies Lee and Perrin's; references to bought puff pastry indicate Jus-rol, and "hard grated cheese" should be, for perfection, Parmesan, and where "melting" type cheese is indicated, it is ideally Emmenthal, the poor relation with the large holes in of Swiss Gruyère which has the small holes in.

"Beer" indicates ordinary draught beer; "light ale" indicates bottled ale and "plonk" is the current term used for the cheapest type of cooking—as specified—wine that you can obtain. If you remind yourselves that fine wine should never be boiled, you will accept that most soups are boiled and therefore fine wines should not be used.

All references to "whipped cream" or "thick cream" indicate a choice between whipping or double cream for you.

References to "potato flour" signify French packet *fécule de pommes de terre*.

Soup Accompaniments and Basics

Diablotins
Pulled Bread
Bouquet Garni
Toast Melba
Garlic Loaf
Frozen Tarragon
Frozen Parsley for Winter Use
Basic White Sauce for Purée Soups
Tortillas
Herby Bread
Frozen Chives for Winter Use
Frikadeller
Drunken Prawns
Chervil Butter
Oignons Royale
Egg and Milk Croûtons
Soubise Sauce
Fried Croûtons
Mrs. Marshall's Cheese Sippets
Seasoned Flour
How to make Buttery Toast with, always, untorn surfaces
Garlic Butter
Thin Soup Velouté
Semolina Dumplings
Liver Dumplings
Tiddeley Pasties
Le Coulis Niçois
Tomato Juice
Fried Parsley
Marrow Toast
Paprika Butter
Cheese Straws

Diablotins

24 ¾ inch thick rounds thinnest   *grated hard cheese.*
    possible French bread (flute),

Heap each baby bread-round with cheese, pass under a slow grill
to bubble. Set on top of each bowlful of either *Pot-au-Feu* and
Consommé de Volaille au Diablotins.

Pulled Bread

This is made with crusts torn from a cottage loaf, or ones from each
end of sandwich loaf plus side crusts, cut off when making sandwiches. Lay on baking sheet, brown in oven at 355 F (gas 4) one
shelf above centre for 7 minutes. Pile into napkin-lined bowl, flip
over napkin corners to keep warm.

Bouquet Garni (Faggot of Herbs)

1 parsley stalk and, when   *2 sprigs thyme,*
    possible, root,   *optional sprig marjoram.*
1 torn bay leaf,

Tie all in muslin with fine string and store in a jar in a dry place.

Toast Melba

Use de-crusted slices from a bought, sliced sandwich loaf. Toast on
both sides; while piping hot split centrally and toast the untoasted
sides. Do not store in a tin as nasty restaurants do and give it to
you stone cold and nearly as old as Methuselah. Serve it fresh, it
is so easy.

Garlic Loaf

There are three types: a) made with miniature brown loaves, in which case allow 1 per person; b) with brown quartern loaves; c) with *flutes*—the long baton-type sticks of French bread.

The method is constant. Slice chosen bread **through to base-crust,** but **not through crust itself.** Thus loaf opens out like a fan. Spread garlic butter (page 18) liberally **between** the fan/cuts, **on both sides.** Press together again. Wrap tightly in aluminium foil. Store until just before service. Then slip into oven 335 F (gas 4) mid shelf for 5 minutes for individual loaves; 10 minutes for large ones. Serve piping hot.

Frozen Tarragon

Strip all the leaves from French tarragon (better flavour than Russian). Chop extremely finely. Treat exactly as for frozen chives, (page 15).

Frozen Parsley for Winter Use

Pick every scrap of stalk from the heads of French or English parsley. Put in a parsley mill, turn the handle vigorously first one way, then in the opposite direction; alternatively chop finely. Treat exactly as explained for frozen chives (page 15).

Note: Do not throw away stalks. Use in stocks or emulsify or liquidise for health food, cold soups or health drinks.

Basic White Sauce for Purée Soups (Béchamel)

*1 oz butter, dripping or dissolved
    pork fat,
1 oz flour,*

*1 pint milk or ½ pint each of
    milk and well reduced stock.*

Soften chosen fat in thick pan. Stir in flour, work to soft ball which leaves sides and base of pan clear. Add heated fluid gradually beating thoroughly between each addition.

Note: Can be made in bulk if desired. Store in ordinary domestic refrigeration. To prevent top-crusting, either pass a hot tablespoon through butter and rub base slightly over surface (Escoffier's way) or cut circle of greaseproof to container's top-size, run under cold tap and press down over sauce surface.

Tortillas

*8 oz cornflour,
½ teaspoonful salt,*

lukewarm water.

Work cornflour with salt and small additions water to form a smooth rolling dough **which is not sticky**! Roll into walnut-sized balls. Roll out very thinly to 4 inch circles. Lay each on waxed paper. Cover with waxed paper, then clean cloth, then heavy weight (cookery books!) for 30 minutes. Peel off and deep fry in hot oil until crisp, drain and serve.

Herby Bread

Treat exactly as for Garlic Bread (page 13) but replace garlic butter with following mixture:

*1 heaped teaspoonful each of
    fresh thyme, parsley, tarragon,
    chervil and chives,*

*3 oz soft butter,
1 crushed garlic clove,
1 flat eggspoonful salt.*

Chop or mill all herbs. Beat butter to cream, beat in herbs, crushed garlic and salt. Use as for Garlic Butter.

Frozen Chives for Winter Use

Scissor finely a large bowlful of fresh green chives. Pack down into the ice-cube compartments of refrigerator trays. Fill up with teaspoonfuls cold water. Freeze. Unmould, bag up in polythene bags. Secure with closures. When required, thaw overnight in small sieve over bowl. In morning chives will only need patting in dry cloth to be ready for service.

Frikadeller (Meat Balls)

4 oz minced lean of raw beef,
1 oz soft white crumbs,
a little milk,
1 teaspoonful potato flour or
  arrowroot,

1 flat teaspoonful salt,
generous pinch black pepper,
1 very small egg yolk.

Work beef, crumbs, seasoning, potato flour or arrowroot, salt and pepper very thoroughly together. Beat in yolk with a few drops milk, add more sparingly to achieve firm dough. Roll into walnut-sized balls. Drop into pan of fast-boiling salted water, simmer for 10 mins. Serve a few in each bowlful of soup.

Drunken Prawns

½ pint prawns,
4 fluid oz dry cooking sherry,
2 dessertspoonsful cold water,

2 dessertspoonsful wine vinegar,
4 dessertspoonsful Soy sauce.

Wash prawns, scissor off legs, drain, dry, place in small pan with sherry. Bring to boil, simmer 3 minutes, drain sherry off prawns and mix it with water, vinegar and Soy. Rest 4 hours. Serve 2/3 to each person, with a little liquor in tiny Chinese saucers to accompany **Three Delicious Soups** (page 92).

Chervil Butter

This is simply creamed butter to which 1 dessertspoonful of fresh chervil is added. The preparation is easier with a herb mill. Otherwise just chop finely and then whisk into creamed butter with salt and pepper to taste. Made in fresh chervil season you can store for a long time in ordinary domestic refrigeration.

Oignons Royale

$2\frac{1}{2}$ oz grated raw onion,
$\frac{1}{2}$ oz butter,
1 tablespoonful Béchamel
   (page 14),
2 separated egg yolks,
$2\frac{1}{2}$ fluid oz thick cream whipped
   stiffly,

1 dessertspoonful raw egg white,
1–2 drops carmine liquid
   colouring,
salt and sugar.

Dissolve butter in little pan. Work in onion and stir while cooking gently until tender. Sieve, work in Béchamel with pinch salt and sugar. Colour lightly. Stir in, off heat, beaten cream yolks and unbeaten egg white. Pour into buttered 6 inch diameter heat-resistant container. Stand in outer meat-baking tin containing 1 inch boiling water and poach until set under foil "lid". Leave until cold. Ease out onto working surface, stamp into tiny fancy shapes or just dice. Use for garnish.

Egg and Milk Croûtons

Stamp $\frac{1}{4}$ inch thick slices of crustless bread into small squares, triangles, fingers or rectangles with plain or scallop-edged cutters. Beat 1 small egg with 4 fluid oz milk and strain. Check oil in deep fryer is ready heated (385 F); tow each piece through egg mixture quickly, slide into hot oil and fry to golden-brown on each side. Drain on absorbent kitchen paper. Hand plain with soups, or spread with herb butters, garlic butter, chopped hard-boiled white or yolk of egg mixed with a little stiff cream and salt and pepper seasoned or anchovy purée, for a few examples.

Soubise Sauce

Simmer ½ lb thinly sliced onions in milk-to-cover liberally. When tender, drain off half remaining milk, set aside, liquidise the rest, return to pan. Simmer remaining milk down to 2 fluid oz, correct seasoning lightly and bring to total half pint with one of the following, a) milk, b) top of milk, c) single or double cream.

Fried Croûtons

1 oz butter,   *3 slices from a sandwich loaf*
1 oz oil,   *(thinly cut) or ¼ inch slices.*

Heat oil and dissolve butter therein. Dice bread small (crusts left on). When pan mixture "sings", toss bread in and have a perforated spoon or metal spatula to hand so that you can shake, stir, turn over strong heat until dice are richly browned and they have taken up every scrap of fat.

Mrs. Marshall's Cheese Sippets

A few remainders of bought or home made puff paste. Mrs. Marshall's Cheese Sauce made with 1½ gills milk and 2 tablespoonsful cream. (See Mrs. M's Remarkable Quick Soup, page 200).

Roll out paste trimming thinly. Lay on a tap-rinsed wet baking sheet. Bake until risen and browned 400 F (gas 6) 1 shelf above centre. Press down risen tops. Place made sauce in nylon non-sweat icing bag with medium "crown" pipe affixed. When sauce is cool enough to handle, pipe little rosettes on to pastry squares, dust tops with powdered paprika and serve with chosen soups.

Seasoned Flour

(Storage quantity for dry goods shelf in airtight tin.)

2 lb self-raising flour,
4 oz salt,
1 oz pepper,
1 oz dry English mustard,
½ oz paprika powder,

1 heaped tablespoonful each of dried tarragon, dried thyme, dried parsley,
1 flat dessertspoonful dried sage,
1 flat teaspoonful powdered bay leaf.

Powder all dry herbs then mix with all remaining ingredients.

Buttery Toast with, always, Untorn Surfaces

(Please do not be offended! We merely pass on Mum's trick which we have found marvellous.)

Soften some butter in a shallow container—like an ordinary Victoria sponge tin. When melted, make toast under full strength grill, set at high position. As each slice is completed, slap down onto melted butter. Lift up, shake off drips and so continue. Do also with little toasted cornflour scones, or any other toasted item which requires buttering.

Garlic Butter

As this will keep indefinitely in refrigeration we give a fairly large (domestic) quantity. Please use a lidded, modern plastic pot or small box for storage to ensure this butter does not contaminate other refrigerator contents.

4 oz cooking type butter,
4 peeled garlic cloves (not to be confused with whole "head of garlic"),

2 generously rounded table-spoonsful freshly milled, fresh parsley heads,
salt and pepper.

18

Whip butter until light and pale, chop peeled garlic cloves and thereafter **crush** with the tip of a small table knife with thumb on blade-tip to reduce to a complete pap. Only thus should garlic be used except for such soups as *Potage des Noces* (page 46). Add garlic and parsley to butter and whip down until thoroughly incorporated. Add a generous pinch of salt and a ¼ flat teaspoonful of white pepper.

Thin Soup Velouté

1 oz dripping or butter,
1 oz flour,

1 pint white stock, i.e. made
from white meat or white
meat bones.

Dissolve chosen fat in thick, small pan. Add flour, work with wooden spoon to make White Roux—a misnomer since it is yellowish! When the two ingredients come together to form a soft ball which leaves sides and base of pan clear, cook over low heat, stirring the while for 3 minutes. Add a quarter of the stock, which is preferably boiling, to save waiting time. As this bubbles in pan, stir to incorporate, finally beat until smooth and repeat using up all given fluid.

Semolina Dumplings

2 oz butter,
salt, pepper,

2 eggs,
scant 3½ oz semolina.

Whip butter until white and very loose, add 2 generous pinches salt, 1 of pepper and whip in semolina gradually. Beat in eggs. **Rest 24 hours** under covering plate. Drop fat teaspoonful into chosen simmering soup. When all are risen serve in soup.

Liver Dumplings

10 oz stale bread (including
crusts),
4 fluid oz boiling milk,
14 oz minced pigs' or chickens'
livers,
2 oz grated onion pap,

2 eggs,
1 flat teaspoonful salt,
¼ flat teaspoonful pepper,
1 scant flat teaspoonful mixed
spice.

Pour milk over roughly torn bread. When thoroughly soaked, squeeze up to pap. Add all remaining ingredients. Shape into small balls. Drop into gently-simmering soup. They will sink. When all are risen, either serve separately or in tureen of chosen soup.

Tiddeley Pasties

Roll out any good shortcrust to ⅛ inch thickness. Stamp into 3½ inch diameter circles. Wet edges, put small heap of diced streaky bacon mixed with a little raw beaten egg in centre of one half of each. Flip over, pinch edges securely together. Brush tops with milk or cream. Bake on lightly-floured sheet, 335 F (gas 4) one shelf above centre, until lightly browned for approximately 16 minutes.

Le Coulis Nicois

1½ fluid oz oil,
4 chopped onions,
1 lb ripe tomatoes,
1 oz flour,
salt and pepper,
2 tarragon heads,

4 fluid oz single cream or
top-of-milk,
1 flat dessertspoonful dry
English mustard,
3 pints strong bone stock,
2 parsley stalks.

Heat oil in frying pan. When "singing" add onions and cook gently until soft but not browned. Stir in flour and mustard to form soft ball, turn into roomy pan, add rough-cut tomatoes, stock, parsley and tarragon. Simmer for 1 hour. Remove herbs. Emulsify, liquidise or sieve, re-heat, stir in cream and correct seasoning.

Tomato Juice

2 lb over-ripe tomatoes,
4 fluid oz chicken stock, (A or
  B page 125),

1 flat teaspoonful powdered
  celery salt.

Place all ingredients in thick pan and stir over moderate flame until tomatoes are collapsed and juices running freely. Press with back of wooden spoon through sieve and use.

Fried Parsley

Select fat parsley heads on very short stalks. Heat oil in deep fryer to 385 F. Wash sprigs. Dry thoroughly in clean cloth. Slip into oil. As each sprig sizzles and crisps, lift out gently with metal lifting tongs, drain and use.

Marrow Toast

Toast thinly-cut sandwich loaf slices on both sides. Spread with marrow excavated from bone. Season strongly with black pepper, lightly with salt and cayenne, cut into fingers for service.

Paprika Butter

4 oz salted butter,
1 heaped tablespoonful paprika
  powder,

1 teaspoonful Masala Paste,
1 generous pinch cayenne.

Beat all ingredients to a bright pink cream. Store in plastic, lidded pot in refrigerator. Keeps indefinitely.

21

Cheese Straws

In these busy, fraught times, we make no apologies for giving you the quick, easy way!

$\frac{1}{4}$ lb bought, frozen puff paste,
1 small, raw, beaten, strained
   egg,
1 teaspoonful olive oil,

salt and white pepper,
1$\frac{1}{4}$ oz Parmesan grated finely,
water.

Roll paste out really thinly. Cut into two 4 inch wide matching rectangles. Brush one all over with egg mixture, i.e. beaten egg blended with oil, and pinch salt and pepper. Scatter with generous two-thirds of the cheese. Roll down very lightly. Brush one side of second half with egg, lay over cheesey panel. Roll gently to make adhere. Cut into strips. Bend 6 strips to form small circles. Egg ends and press together. Brush all tops with egg, scatter over remaining cheese. Bake at 400 F (gas 6) 1 shelf above centre until golden brown. Serve hot. Stuff 2/3 straws into each ring for show-off!

Meal-In-Itself Soups

1. Garbure
2. Left-over Version of Garbure
3. Croûte-au-Pot
4. Elzekaria
5. Minestronis
6. Gul Artsoppa Kungsholm
7. Purée Conti   ——————
8. Hunter's Pot
9. Braunschweiger Fruhlinggsuppe Griefsklofsen
10. Scots' Barley Broth
11. Bableves Csipetkevel
12. Mixed Vegetable Pot
13. Cabbage and Chipolata Pot
14. Erwtensoep

1 Garbure (Vegetable Soup from the Bearn)

¼ lb raw gammon,
3 large old peeled potatoes,
3 medium, trimmed or 2 large
  leeks,
3 scraped carrots,
6 bacon rinds or gammon rind,
1 green or red pimento,
1 rounded teaspoon paprika
  powder,
3 peeled garlic cloves,
1 peeled turnip,
1 large sprig dried or fresh
  marjoram,

1 large sprig dried or fresh
  thyme,
2 dried or fresh basil leaves,
1 small tight white or green
  cabbage,
½ lb overnight-soaked dried
  peas,
½ lb overnight-soaked dried
  butter beans,
1 thin slice brown bread per
  serving.

Place gammon in large glazed earthenware casserole. Fill to within 1 inch of top with boiling water. When bubbling toss in rough-cut potatoes, cleaned 1 inch leek pieces, strained peas, strained beans, turnip cut into 8 sections, sliced carrots, chosen pimento halved and cut into strips with all pith and pips removed. Raise again to boiling, add paprika, marjoram, thyme, basil and peeled rough-crushed garlic cloves, and simmer steadily. When dried beans are firm and not quite cooked, add cabbage cut into hair-thin strips and bacon rinds. Cover and cook in oven at 310 F (gas 2), 1 shelf below centre for 2½ hours.

Just before serving, remove bacon and herb sprigs, dice up bacon finely and keep warm separately. Stir soup and season to taste.

For service, place a slice of brown bread in each soup bowl. Fill up with pot mixture and pass round diced bacon for each person to stir into their Garbure. If wanting to show off, ask everyone to eat the thickest part of this brew LEAVING SOME LIQUOR in base of each bowl. Serve each with a half-filled glass of a humble, fairly strong red wine and stir into remaining soup.

2 Left-over version of Garbure

Any remainders of Garbure (see above) will be very thick indeed so dilute to required consistency with stock, heat through and, at moment of service, split fat, 4/5 inch wedges from a French loaf.

Toast the bread, then spread with butter and sprinkle thickly with Gruyère or Emmenthal cheese. Return to grill until bubbling and brown. Pour re-heated soup into old-fashioned soup plates, thereby breaking our general rule—float toasted French bread on top, serve as filling supper dish.

3 Croûte-au-Pot

This very old French recipe is inexpensive, extremely filling and well-worth the little bit of care required. Make a mental note to make the next time you have the requisite chicken, duck or goose fat available.

1 small white cabbage,
2 large, lengthwise quartered
  carrots,
1 large onion,
4 cloves,
1 peeled garlic clove,

salt and pepper,
6 pints strained pork-bone
  stock,
4 oz melted chicken, duck or
  goose fat,
2 very small cottage loaves.

Blanch cabbage, carrots and onion by immersing in boiling water and leaving 10 minutes. Quarter cabbage, stick onion with cloves, put crushed garlic clove into large pot or pan, with stock. Run chosen fat over top-surface, simmer 2 hours with light seasoning of salt and pepper. Cut base crusts from both little loaves. Pull out all interior crumb. Spoon off into small bowl as much of poultry fat as possible. Then strain pan contents, put vegetables (removing onion's cloves) into lidded dish and keep warm. Return liquor to clean pan. Plunge in each hollowed bread case until well-impregnated. Lift out and set both side by side on a meat baking tin. Pour over skimmed-off fat. Put into oven at 400 F (gas 6) to become crip and browned.

Remove onto heated dish, pile in vegetables. Pour liquor into a tureen. Each person takes some vegetables, a wedge of baked bread crust and adds to a big bowl of liquor. Optionally hand hard, grated cheese in another bowl.

4 Elzekaria (typical Meal-In-Itself Soup from the Pays Basque)

3 oz melted pork or goose fat,
1 large thinly sliced onion,
1 extremely small, tight white
  cabbage, sliced thinly,
1 pint overnight-soaked butter
  beans,

2 crushed garlic cloves,
salt and pepper,
1 large chopped sage leaf,
1 sprig thyme or oregano,
5 pints strong bone stock,
wine vinegar.

Heat fat until "singing" in large pan. Fry onions gently until soft but not browned. Add cabbage, stir/fry 5 minutes, work in garlic, turn into lidded casserole (for oven) saucepan (for top-burner) add beans, herbs, 1 generous teaspoonful salt and all given stock. Simmer 2 hours or casserole under lid in oven 310 F (gas 2) 1 shelf below centre, for 3½ hours. Remove, uncover and skim off surplus top-floating fat with absorbent kitchen papers. Just tow across and discard. Serve in large, heated bowls. Hand small jug wine vinegar for each person to drip in few drops and stir before eating. Optionally hand Herby Bread (page 14) separately.

5 Minestronis (Sardinian Vegetable Soup with Pigs' Ears. A Meal-In-Itself)

4 oz chopped French beans,
4 oz small broad beans,
4 oz shredded spring cabbage,
4 oz raw diced potato,
1 sprig fennel,
2 scrubbed, singed pigs' ears
  (unsalted),

2 oz diced raw pork fat,
salt and pepper,
1 flat teaspoonful chopped fresh
  or crumbled dried basil,
4 very ripe, peeled tomatoes,
  diced,
5 pints good bone stock.

Put everything except seasonings into roomy pan and simmer 3½ hours. Excavate pigs' ears. Remove all small bones. Cut up skin and flesh into minute cubes. Return these to soup, taste, season strongly and serve with grated hard cheese and fried croûtons (page 17).

26

6 Gul Artsoppa Kungsholm (Scandinavian Split Pea and Pork Meal-In-Itself-Soup)

12 oz split dried yellow peas,
1 lb salt pork or unsoaked
* gammon,*
1 large thinly sliced leek,

¼ flat teaspoonful powdered
* ginger,*
salt and pepper,
4 pints white bone stock.

Soak peas overnight in cold water. Drain, put into roomy pan, cover with boiling stock, simmer steadily for 10 minutes. Meanwhile immerse pork or gammon in separate bowl of boiling water for 10 minutes. Drain and sink into simmering soup with leek. Simmer gently 2 hours. Correct seasoning, add ginger, simmer 4 minutes. Skim carefully with absorbent kitchen paper. Slice meat and arrange on heated dish. Hand plenty of crusty bread.

Alternatively immerse meat in soup and serve in large old-fashioned soup plates, with made English mustard. This is for English tastes, so a separate dish of plain, steamed potatoes may be added.

7 Purée Conti (Filling family soup, extremely warming in cold weather)

¾ lb lentils,
2 oz lean breast of bacon or
* gammon,*
1 quart good pork, beef or
* mutton bone stock,*

3 oz diced carrot,
1 medium, diced onion,
1 bouquet garni,
pepper,
1 walnut of butter.

Set lentils in roomy bowl and cover with luke-warm water. Soak 2 hours. Dice bacon, set in roomy pan, add strained lentils, carrot, onion, herbs, stock and bring to boil gently, skim, simmer 1 hour. Remove bouquet garni, emulsify or sieve. Dilute to required consistency with a) further stock, or b) milk. Taste, correct seasoning, stir in butter in flakes, serve with fried croûtons (page 17).

8 Hunter's Pot

This is a dish which we ate as children after duck-shooting on the Norfolk Broads. It is the most filling of inexpensive soups and, when bitterly cold, it becomes a gastronomic hot-water bottle for limited incomes.

3 quarts good clear bone soup,
2 lb thinly sliced onions,
½ lb very thinly-sliced, stale Cheddar cheese,

salt and pepper to season,
1 sandwich loaf cut in slices with crusts left on,
butter to spread slices.

Take a very large pot, pan or casserole WITH NO HANDLE. Line base with bread slices, buttered side downwards. Cover with layer of onions. Season, cover with a layer of cheese and repeat until the pot is just under half-full. Press down as hard as you can. Prod a large hole in centre using a well-scrubbed finger or the handle of a wooden spoon. Put boiling stock into kettle, hold as high above the container as possible, and pour through the hole until the whole island of bread, onions and cheese shifts and rises to top of pan. Cover with lid or kitchen foil, place in oven at 310 F (gas 2). Cook for at least 4 hours. When you have eaten this, if you are still hungry, we give up!

9 Braunschweiger Fruhlinggsuppe Griefsklofsen (Brunswick Meal-In-Itself Soup with Dumplings)

2 fat beef bones containing marrow,
1 lb shin of beef,
1 lb freshly shelled peas,
8 oz red part only of spring carrots,
1 very small trimmed cauliflower,

6 oz open cup mushrooms or stalks,
1 bouquet garni,
1 large Spanish onion,
1 heaped tablespoonful milled parsley,
salt and pepper,
Semolina Dumplings (page 19).

Rough-cut meat, place in roomy pot or pan with bones, herbs and rough-chopped onion. Cover liberally with cold water, bring to boil, skim carefully, refresh with teacup of cold water, re-raise to boiling, set at simmer, maintain 2½ hours. Add diced white and green of cauliflower, sliced un-skinned mushrooms, diced carrot and peas. Simmer until tender. Taste, correct seasoning, stir in parsley, excavate meat and bones then return to moderate heat. Dice meat, scoop marrow from bones, chop small, stir all into soup, drop in dumplings which will sink. When all rise to top, serve.

Note: Germans hand additional bowl of rough-cut, steamed potatoes.

---

10 Scots' Barley Broth (a Meal-In-Itself Soup)

3 lb fatless scrag end of mutton,	*1 oz dripping,*
1 large rough-cut turnip,	*1 heaped teaspoonful salt,*
1 large rough-cut carrot,	*1 heaped teaspoonful pepper,*
1 trimmed, cleaned celery root,	*2 oz overnight soaked dried*
6 oz overnight-soaked pearl	*peas,*
barley,	*1 fat sprig thyme,*
4 pints mutton bone stock,	*thinly sliced white of 2 large*
2 oz overnight-soaked white	*leeks,*
beans,	*2 medium onions stuck with*
1 oz flour,	*4 cloves.*

Cut mutton up roughly, place in roomy pot or pan with turnip, carrot, celery, leeks, onions. Cover with stock, boil, skim and then simmer 2 hours. Excavate meat, remove all bones, cut up small. Add peas, beans and barley to soup and simmer on for 30 minutes. Meanwhile, heat dripping in small pan, stir in flour to soft ball stage, dilute with small ladleful soup, stir very thoroughly, repeat, and when mixture is creamy and thick, stir back into soup. Fish out onions, remove cloves, chop and return with thyme. Simmer 8 more minutes. Taste and correct seasoning. Fish out thyme for service.

11 Bableves Csipetkevel (Hungarian Bean Soup; a Meal-In-Itself-Soup)

5 oz dried, white beans soaked
   overnight,
1 large diced onion,
2 quarts strong bone stock,
2 large diced carrots,
1 diced parsnip,
4 oz dripping or dissolved pork
   fat,
6½ oz sifted flour,

1 flat dessertspoonful salt,
1 rounded teaspoonful paprika
   powder,
1 egg,
2 tablespoonsful water,
3 Hungarian frankfurters or
   2 Czechoslovakian
   frankfurters.

Place strained beans in large pot or pan with stock, carrots, and parsnip. Boil, skim, simmer 2 hours. Excavate 1 teacupful beans, sieve, emulsify or liquidise with a little of liquor. Return purée to pan. Heat pork fat, fry onion briskly and ALLOW TO BROWN. Work in 2 just-rounded tablespoonsful given flour and the paprika. When pasty add ½ pint pot liquor, gradually beating between each addition. Scrape all into soup. Simmer extremely gently for 1 hour stirring occasionally to avoid base catching. Put remaining flour in bowl, make central well break in egg and water and work to smooth paste. Turn onto floured, cold surface, knead, adding extra flour siftings until dough is smooth and no longer sticky. Roll out extremely thinly. Leave exposed 45 minutes. Cut dough into 1 inch squares. Raise nearly-finished soup to strong boil, stir to ensure no-catching, drop in dough squares. When all are risen to top of soup, stir in chosen frankfurters sliced thinly and previously fried 4 minutes in hot butter and oil.

12 Mixed Vegetable Pot (A Meal-In-Itself-Soup)

5 large, thinly sliced leaves of
   Savoy cabbage,
6 oz coarse-grated carrot,
6 oz coarse-grated onion,
1 thinly sliced, fat leek,
4 oz overnight-soaked dried
   peas,
1 rounded tablespoonful
   concentrated tomato purée,

4 sage leaves chopped or
   1 teaspoonful dried sage,
6 bacon rinds,
1 garlic clove (optional),
5 pints strong stock,
1 flat dessertspoonful salt,
1 scant flat teaspoonful pepper,
1 bouquet garni.

Put all ingredients into lidded pot or pan. Bring to boil, simmer steadily under lid 2½ hours. Optionally stir in 4 oz *stellete* (star-shaped) pasta, or alphabetical pasta. Hand grated cheese and fried croûtons (page 17). Remember to fish out herbs and bacon rinds before serving.

13 Cabbage and Chipolata Pot (A Meal-In-Itself-Soup)

1½ lb very thinly-sliced white
  cabbage,
1 lb very thinly-sliced onion,
1 bouquet garni,
1 level dessertspoonful salt,
1 scant, flat teaspoonful pepper,

4½ pints strongly reduced stock,
½ pint beer,
¼ lb chipolatas,
1 heaped tablespoonful paprika
  powder.

Put stock into roomy, lidded casserole, add cabbage, onions, herbs, salt, pepper. Cover, put in oven 355 F (gas 4) mid-shelf for 3 hours. Mix paprika to thin paste with beer. Pour into soup, stir. Add cooked, sliced chipolata rounds, remove herbs, return to oven 15 minutes. Hand grated cheese and Pulled Bread (page 12) separately.

14 Erwtensoep (Dutch National Soup. A Meal-In-Itself)

¼ lb overnight-soaked split peas,
5 pints water or bone stock,
2 unsalted pig's trotters.
1 fat marrow bone,
¼ lb thinly sliced old potatoes,
sliced white and green of 3
  medium leeks,

3 sliced, outside sticks celery,
salt and pepper,
4 sliced frankfurters,
1 rounded tablespoonful milled,
  fresh parsley heads,
3 medium onions sliced thinly.

Simmer trotters and bone in roomy pan with stock for 1 hour. Add strained, soaked peas, simmer on 1 hour. Add all vegetables, and simmer on 35 minutes. Excavate marrow bone and trotters. Scoop out marrow, chop and return to soup. Bone and chop trotters and add also. Taste, correct seasoning, stir in parsley and frankfurters. When soup is boiling and frankfurters are hot, serve with hunks cut from crusty cottage loaf.

Vegetable Soups

15. Emergency Celery Soup (from a tin!)
16. Piquante Tomato Soup (hot)
17. Simple Milk Vegetable Soup B
18. Simple Vegetable Soup A
19. Family Pea Soup
20. Split Pea Soup
21. Sauerkraut Soup
22. Modest Mushroom Soup
23. Simple Onion Soup
24. Brown Celery Soup with Croûtons
25. Vegetable Soup with Rice
26. Brussels Sprouts and Chestnut Soup
27. Simple Chicken and Corn Soup
28. Watercress and Spring Onion Soup
29. Curried Pea and Avocado Soup
30. Pan Kail
31. Red Cabbage Soup
32. Haricot Bean Soup
33. Creole Lenten Soup
34. Family Soup from Boiled Gammon Liquor
35. Cabbage Soup 1
36. Barbecue Soup

15 Emergency Celery Soup (from a tin!)

Empty the contents of a large tin of celery hearts into your liquidiser or emulsifier and reduce to pulp. Rub through a sieve. Stir in 1½ pints milk in pan over low heat. Add 2 oz grated hard cheese (ideally Parmesan), allow to come to boiling point, taste, correct seasoning and if possible, just before serving, run a little single or double cream over the back of a dessertspoon held just above the soup line of each bowlful.

16 Piquante Tomato Soup (Hot)

½ pint tomato coulis (below),
½ pint chicken stock A (page 125),
1 heaped teaspoonful each of
  milled parsely heads and of
  scissored chives,

1½ oz stiffly whipped whipping
  cream,
salt and pepper.

Blend stock and *coulis*, raise to boiling point, correct seasoning. Blend three-quarters of given herbs into cream. Float blobs on top of each serving and scatter remainder of herbs overall.

Tomato coulis is a basic, keeping sauce for which, when tomatoes are at low summer price you rough cut 4 lb well ripened ones. Put in 10 heads each of fresh thyme and tarragon; 1½ oz chopped chives and 6 crushed garlic cloves. Simmer to pulp, sieve, put back into pan, stir in 8 tablespoonsful olive oil, blend, bottle and sterilise for storage.

17 Simple Milk Vegetable Soup (B)

1 large carrot,
1 medium onion,
4 over-large brussels sprouts and
  2 medium potatoes, all
  coarse-grated,
2 pints milk or 1 pint each milk
  and white bone stock,
1 oz dripping,

1 oz flour,
2 oz overnight soaked pearl
  barley,
salt and pepper,
1 sprig thyme,
2 heads tarragon,   ⎫ all tied
½ torn bay leaf,   ⎬ into
1 tiny blade mace.   ⎭ muslin.

Place grated vegetables and milk or milk and stock in pan with herb bag. Bring to boil, simmer 1 hour. Dissolve dripping, work in flour to soft ball, add strained soup liquor gradually beating well between each addition. Return to vegetable pan, remove herb bag, add barley, simmer 10 minutes, serve with Fried Croûtons (page 17) or Pulled Bread (page 12) and an optional bowl of grated hard cheese, ideally Parmesan.

Note: This soup is also good with a sprinkling of coarse-grated Emmenthal in the base of each heated bowl before pouring on soup.

18 Simple Vegetable Soup (A)

1 large carrot,
1 large onion, coarse grated,
shredded white and green of
*   1 leek,*
3 pints strong bone stock,

3 rounded tablespoonsful
*   broken-up vermicelli,*
1 rounded tablespoonful
*   concentrated tomato purée,*
salt, pepper and a herb faggot.

Place herb faggot, carrot, onion, leek and bone stock in pan, bring to boil, skim, then simmer 1 hour. Add vermicelli, cook for 5 more minutes, stir in purée, correct seasoning, fish out herb bag before service.

19 Family Pea Soup

1 pint split peas, soaked
*   overnight in cold water to*
*   cover,*
1 herb faggot,
1 breakfastcupful finely-sliced
*   white and green of leeks,*

6 bacon rinds,
2 raw, unsalted pig's trotters,
$\frac{1}{2}$ a small pig's head,
5 pints well-reduced bone stock,
$\frac{1}{4}$ lb skinned, diced smoked
*   sausage.*

Put drained soaked peas into roomy pan with pig's trotters and stock, pig's head, herbs, bacon rinds and leeks. Simmer for 3 hours over low heat **and** asbestos mat. Alternatively, casserole in bottom of slow oven under lid, until flesh falls from head piece and trotters. Fish out rinds and discard. Then remove head piece and trotters. Peel away all skin, chop up remainder, return to soup, emulsify or sieve, season lightly with salt, strongly with pepper and stir in sausage dice.

Optionally hand bowl of grated hard cheese separately. Remember this soup re-heats superbly.

20 Split Pea Soup

½ lb dry split peas,
1 quart water,
1 quart well-reduced stock,
2 parsley stalks,

1 small, thinly cut strip lemon
  peel,
12 bacon rinds,
one 3 oz piece lean raw bacon
  or gammon.

Soak peas overnight in water. Strain and discard water. Place all ingredients in stock, bring to boil, skim, simmer until sufficiently tender for all to be rubbed through sieve. Correct seasoning with pepper only. If considered too thick, dilute with milk or top-of-the-milk. Serve with little fried diced bread croûtons.

21 Sauerkraut Soup

8 oz tinned or home-made
  sauerkraut,
1 quart strong beef bone stock,
3 oz lean gammon,
4 medium tomatoes,
1 rounded dessertspoonful
  freshly-milled parsley,

1 standard carton soured
  cream,
pepper,
½ oz butter,
½ oz olive oil.

Heat butter with oil and fry sauerkraut until distinctly browned. Put gammon with one third of stock in roomy pan, cover and simmer 35 minutes. Fish out gammon, add rough cut, skinned tomatoes and sauerkraut. Simmer on 20 minutes with gammon cut into fine strips. At moment of service stir in soured cream and parsley, correct seasoning.

22 Modest Mushroom Soup

1 lb finely chopped mushrooms
and their stalks,
2 oz finely chopped shallots,
1 very small crushed garlic
clove,
1¼ oz butter,
1½ oz flour,

1½ pints white bone stock,
¼ pint dry white wine,
salt, pepper and nutmeg to
season,
¼ pint top-of-the-milk or cream,
1½ fluid oz olive oil.

Heat oil and butter together in a thick shallow pan. Add shallots and cook gently for 3 minutes. Add prepared mushrooms and garlic. Continue cooking gently over low heat until all are tender. Stir in flour, work to rough paste with the back of a wooden spoon. Add wine gradually, stirring well between each addition. Turn into a saucepan, add heated stock gradually, stirring continuously. Simmer for 30 minutes stirring occasionally, then taste, correct seasoning, stir in chosen cream and reheat when required.

23 Simple Onion Soup

3 pints of cleared bone stock,
1 tablespoonful flour,
salt,
ground black peppercorns,
grated cheese,

1 lb peeled chopped onion,
garlic clove (optional),
a few bread crusts,
2 oz dripping.

Heat dripping in a shallow pan and fry onions and crushed garlic over low heat until tender. Work in flour and add stock gradually until mixture is just thick and very smooth. Then scrape into a saucepan and stir in the remaining liquor. Allow to simmer very gently for a further 30 minutes, giving only an occasional stir. Taste, correct seasoning and when serving, fill into bowls, float a piece of toasted crust on top of each, cover with a heaped dessert-spoonful grated stale cheese and bubble under grill, so remember to use heat-resistant soup bowls whenever possible. If your bowls are NOT heat-resistant make double bands of aluminium foil to press all round rims and thus protect rims from grill.

24 Brown Celery Soup with Croûtons

4 pints of cleared bone stock,
1 trimmed head of celery,
3 oz grated stale Cheddar
   cheese,
salt and pepper,

1 very flat teaspoonful celery
   salt,
¾ inch slices of (preferably)
   brown bread,
1 oz each of butter and oil.

Wash the celery, removing the leaf ends and any dark green. Chop the rest finely, toss into the stock in a roomy pan and simmer until celery is just tender. Emulsify or liquefy back into pan. Stir in cheese and seasonings to taste, add the celery salt and at the moment of service, fry croûtons (page 17) and hand separately.

25 Vegetable Soup with Rice

4 pints cold water,
8 oz trimmed sliced carrots,
6 oz cleaned trimmed!green and
   white of leeks,
1 sprig rosemary,
1 flat teaspoonful dried thyme,

1 small torn bay leaf,
2 peppercorns,
6 oz diced raw potatoes,
3 oz rice,
salt and pepper.

Put all ingredients except potatoes and rice into a lidded casserole and cook for 9 hours at 240 F (gas ¼) on bottom shelf or for 2 hours 335 F (gas 3) mid-shelf. Add potatoes and rice. Simmer until both are tender. Season with salt and serve with or without a bowl of grated cheese.

Alternatively, after the potatoes and rice are cooked, liquidise, emulsify or sieve to obtain a thicker type of soup.

26 Brussels Sprouts and Chestnut Soup

Strictly speaking this is a Boxing Day Left-over Soup; but those who wish can make it from scratch. The most popular of all Christmas vegetables in our experience is provided by this mixture.

For it, nick, boil until tender, skin and rough-chop ½ lb chestnuts and steam 10 oz small whole or larger halved or quartered Brussels sprouts. When both are cooked and cold, dissolve 2 oz fat from

38

roasted bird in roomy frying pan. When "singing", mix both vegetables together, slide in and fry briskly until well brown (soft fried to a pap these are DISGUSTING!). The mixture must be nutty and crisp. Place in emulsifier with $\frac{1}{4}$ pint very strongly reduced poultry bone stock to every $\frac{1}{4}$ lb. When emulsified or liquidised, place in saucepan, dilute with milk to required consistency, correct seasoning. If 1–2 tablespoonsful cream can be added, so much the better!

---

27 Simple Chicken and Corn Soup

1 small tin well-drained corn,
3 oz minced or finely chopped
  white of celery,
1 pint chicken stock A or B
  (page 125),
4 oz finely chopped, cooked
  white of chicken,

$\frac{1}{2}$ pint milk,
salt and pepper,
tiny pinch cayenne pepper,
2 fluid oz top of milk or single
  cream.

Heat corn in own liquor. Emulsify with a little of given stock and prepared celery. Turn all onto remaining stock in a saucepan, bring to boil then simmer for 15/20 minutes. Add chicken and milk, re-simmer for a moment or two, correct seasoning, add cayenne pepper. Stir in cream and serve.

---

28 Watercress and Spring Onion Soup

2 bunches watercress,
1 bunch spring onions (16 slim
  ones),
12 oz diced potatoes,
1 pint really strong stock,

1 pint milk,
1 teacup top-of-milk or single
  cream,
salt and pepper.

Remove all leaves from watercress. Place stems with potatoes in a roomy pan with stock, simmer 25 minutes. Remove stalks, add milk, spring onions trimmed and chopped. Simmer on until these are tender, add watercress leaves, simmer 2 minutes, then sieve, taste, correct seasoning and add top-of-milk or cream.

29 Curried Pea and Avocado Soup

2 oz finely chopped shallots,
1 flat teaspoonful Masala Paste,
1 fluid oz butter,
1 fluid oz oil,
1 lb shelled peas,
1 flat teaspoonful chervil,

1 pint chicken stock (A or B
  page 125),
1 small avocado,
8 fluid oz single cream or
  top-of-milk,
salt and white pepper.

Heat butter with oil. When "singing", soft-fry shallots gently. When tender add peas, chervil, stock and simmer 25 minutes, stir in Masala Paste then liquidise, emulsify or sieve back into pan. Also sieve peeled avocado flesh. Blend well into soup, add boiling chosen cream and season. Optionally top-garnish with floating "petals" of extra avocado.

30 Pan Kail

4 pints beef bone stock,
3 oz dripping,
1 very small shredded cabbage,

1 oz medium or coarse oatmeal,
salt and pepper.

Dissolve dripping in chosen pan, add cabbage, fry gently, turning occasionally for 5 minutes. Add stock, boil, simmer 30 minutes. Stir in oatmeal, simmer further 30 minutes, taste, correct seasoning, serve and hand Pulled Bread (page 12) separately.

31 Red Cabbage Soup

Use red cabbage instead of given white in Cabbage Soup No. 1 (page 42), otherwise follow recipe, omitting optional sprinkling of cheese but adding 1 fluid oz wine vinegar and 1 heaped teaspoonful soft brown sugar at the last.

32 Haricot Bean Soup

½ lb overnight soaked white
 beans,
2½ pints well-reduced pork bone
 stock,
1 large coarse-grated onion,
1 large coarse-grated carrot,

3 oz dripping or melted pork
 fat,
6 fluid oz top-of-milk or single
 cream,
salt and pepper,
nutmeg.

Melt and heat chosen fat in frying pan. Stir/fry onion, add carrot over moderate heat, cook 5 minutes maximum. Turn into roomy pan, add stock, beans, simmer very strongly until beans are tender. Sieve, emulsify or liquidise. Return to pan, stir in cream when boiling, taste, correct seasoning and add generous grating of nutmeg.

33 Creole Lenten Soup

1 pint overnight soaked split
 peas,
3 pints any bone stock,
1 finely-chopped onion,
1 tablespoonful melted pork or
 chicken fat,
¼ Cos lettuce, shredded,
½ small celery head, sliced,
1 teaspoonful castor sugar,

1 small diced carrot,
2 small diced turnips,
1 fistful spinach leaves,
1 sprig mint,
1 sprig thyme,
1 parsley stalk,
salt and pepper.

Simmer all vegetables except lettuce with herbs in stock until tender, add lettuce, pork fat and sugar. Simmer just until lettuce is really collapsed. Shred lettuce finely, return to pan, correct seasoning, serve with grated cheese and fried croûtons (page 17).

34 Family Soup From Boiled Gammon Liquor

*3 pints stock from cooking
   gammon, ham or bacon,
½ pint milk,
4 outside celery stalks,
1 eggspoonful celery seeds,
1 small coarse-grated onion,
1 rasher finely diced lean bacon,*

*1 bouquet garni,
pepper,
3 oz lightly-broken vermicelli,
   spaghetti or alphabetical
   noodles,
½ lb overnight-soaked split,
   dried peas.*

Place soaked peas in bacon stock and simmer until collapsed with *bouquet garni*, celery seeds, chopped celery and onion. Remove herbs, emulsify, liquidise or sieve, return to clean pan, add bacon and chosen pasta. Simmer 10 minutes, add milk, raise to boiling point, taste, add pepper. Serve with Pulled Bread (page 12).

35 Cabbage Soup 1

*1 lb 2 oz finely shredded cabbage
   (grate in stalks),
2 large or 4 small carrots, diced,
1 leek, shredded
1 lean bacon rasher,*

*1 rounded dessertspoonful
   milled parsley,
2 crushed garlic cloves,
salt and pepper,
3 pints strong bone stock.*

Bring stock to boil, stir in vegetables and simmer 25 minutes. Drain, letting liquor fall back into pan. Chop cabbage finely, return with garlic, parsley, diced bacon and a generous seasoning of pepper. Simmer for further 20 minutes. Optionally sprinkle 1 dessertspoonful grated hard cheese over each bowlful.

36 Barbecue Soup

2 crushed garlic cloves,
4 fluid oz Soy sauce,
2 oz fresh or tinned pineapple
  pulp,
2 oz hair-thin cut carrot,
2 oz hair-thin cut turnip,
2 oz hair-thin cut potato,
1 teaspoonful. Worcestershire
  Sauce,

4 drops Tabasco,
strained juice and grated rind
  1 small orange,
1 quart strongly reduced bone
  stock,
salt and pepper,
4 over-ripe sieved tomatoes.

Simmer potato, garlic, carrots and turnips in stock 5 minutes.
Blend in all other ingredients. Correct seasoning. Serve with side-
dish of hot Chinese Bean Sprouts.

Potages et Purées

37. Potage Familiale No. 1
38. Potage de Noces
39. Potage Frankfurt
40. Purée Parmentier
41. Potage de Poireaux
42. Potage Soissonaise
43. Potage Esau
44. Purée de Celeri-Rave
45. Purée Printanier
46. Purée de Carottes
47. Purée de Panais
48. Purée St. Germain
49. Purée de Laitues 1
50. La Soupe des Vendages
51. Purée de Laitues 2
52. Soupe Maigre
53. Purée Nesselrode
54. Purée Creçy
55. Purée de Tomates
56. Purée Flamande
57. Summer Vegetable Soup from the Bearn
58. Potage aux Endives
59. Potage Maigre
60. Potage Sigurd
61. Peasant Potage St. Germain
62. Potage Madelaine
63. Potage Potiron Basquaise
64. Potage Carlton
65. Potage à la Poissonière
66. Potage aux Haricots Verts
67. Potage Cultivateur

37 Potage Familiale No. 1

These are the backbone of small, honest French restaurants—and are known more often than not as *Potages Pour Les Employées*, but can be obtained by paying clients IF THEY ASK. They are always fresh and innocent of frozen vegetables.

3 quarts any good, cleared bone stock,
1 lb chopped onions,
4 parsley stalks,
1 bouquet garni,
1 lb red part of old carrots, diced,
white and green of 2 finely-sliced leeks,

2 large or 4 small peeled, rough-chopped tomatoes,
1 lb diced potatoes,
1 heaped tablespoonful freshly milled parsley,
salt and pepper,
2 large peeled, crushed garlic cloves,
2 oz dripping.

Heat dripping in roomy frying pan and fry all vegetables gently for 7 minutes. Scrape into large saucepan, cover with stock, sink in *bouquet garni*, add parsley stalks, crushed garlic and bring to the boil. Skim thoroughly and simmer 2 hours. Taste, correct seasoning.

We like to serve this in large, heated bowls with a generous spoonful of any melting-type cheese in the bottom, ideally Gruyère or Emmenthal. Scatter milled parsley over each serving and hand masses of hot French bread cut in slant-wise wedges from a French "flute".

Note: Quite the best liquor for this type of soup is a plain beef-stock residue from boiling what used to be a silverside and is now, because of the cost, a brisket.

38 Potage de Noces

This honeymoon soup comes from the Perigord, where it is served exclusively to honeymooners on their first night. There is no smell of garlic from it, simply because, used in such quantity and in such a manner, this is nullified. It retains certain (alleged) other properties.

12 large, peeled garlic cloves,
2¼ pints chicken stock
(page 125),
1 bouquet garni which must
include both bay leaf and
thyme,
2 separated egg yolks,

1 tablespoonful olive oil,
salt and pepper,
1 tablespoonful brandy,
1 tablespoonful Curaçao.

Put stock and garlic with herb faggot into a casserole, cover and cook for 1½ hours at 310 F (gas 2). Beat egg yolks lightly with a fork, then beat in oil. Remove soup from oven and herbs from soup. Rub soup through a sieve, and re-heat to boiling point. Pour some on to yolks, stir fast, scrape back into pot and stir very thoroughly off the heat. Correct seasoning, add brandy and Curaçao. Serve in deep, heated bowls, wrapped around with white napkins.

Note: Traditionally this soup (see also Soupe de la Nuit de Noce, page 160), is served in bed—extension of the ancient custom of "bundling".

39 Potage Frankfurt

3½ pints cleared chicken stock
(page 125),
8 oz steamed, sieved old
potatoes,
one 6 oz bunch sprew (young
thin asparagus),

4 oz cooked white of chicken
cut in hair-thin strips,
3 fluid oz dry white cooking
wine.

Put prepared chicken stock in roomy pan, bring to boiling point. Cut tips from sprew. Cut off stalks, simmer in stock 20 minutes. Strain, scrape all pulp from sprew stalks, and stir this back into soup with potatoes. When clear, just keep hot. Put sprew tips into small pan with wine, simmer until tender. Strain over soup, stir in liquor, when piping hot, pour into bowls, garnish each serving with chicken strips and sprew tips. Optionally, stir in 4 fluid oz boiling, single cream.

40 Purée Parmentier

This is the original, classic Potato Soup of the great Escoffier. We have merely modified quantities and replaced the given **real** and **costly consommé** with good strong bone stock, cleared and well reduced.

the white of two medium leeks,
1 oz dripping or butter,
10 thinly peeled, rough-sliced,
*   old potatoes,*

1 pint very strongly reduced
*   (flavoursome) white bone*
*   stock,*
extra milk.

Ideally, mince two white of leeks, otherwise chop finely. Fry in heated, chosen fat in medium-sized saucepan. After 4 minutes stir in stock, slice in potatoes and cook rather quickly until potatoes collapse when prodded. Sieve or emulsify. Dilute with additional milk to desired consistency, correct seasoning and, ideally, add a scattering of chopped fresh chervil (when in season) to each serving.

41 Potage de Poireaux

1 lb white and pale green of
*   leeks washed and sliced thinly,*
1 oz butter,.
1 oz oil,

1½ oz grated stale cheese (the
*   classic one is Parmesan),*
salt and pepper,
1 pint Soup Velouté
*   (page 19).*

Pour boiling water over prepared leeks. Leave 2 minutes, drain, wipe and fry in heated and dissolved butter and oil. Fry gently until soft but not browned. Turn into pan, stir in Béchamel and cheese. Simmer extremely gently for 10 minutes, stirring occasionally, then emulsify and correct seasoning to taste.

Note: You can also add 4 fluid oz single cream and serve with fresh, or thawed out frozen, chopped chervil scattered over each bowlful.

42 Potage Soissonaise

1 lb haricot beans soaked
   overnight in cold water to
   cover,
1 large carrot,
1 medium onion,
1½ pints white bone stock,

2 egg yolks,
1 nut of butter,
2 tablespoonsful top-of-milk,
salt and pepper,
1 herb faggot.

Coarse-grate carrot and onion, put in roomy pan with herbs, stock and rinsed beans. Simmer until beans are tender, remove herb faggot, emulsify or sieve. Return to heat, bring to boil, remove from heat. Mix top-of-milk and egg yolks, pour on a little soup stir well, scrape back into bulk of soup (off heat), stir well, season to taste and finally stir in butter.

43 Potage Esau

3 pints cleared mutton bone
   stock,
1 lb red lentils,
4 finely sliced shallots or 2 small
   onions,

5 fluid oz single cream or
   top of the milk,
6 bacon rinds,
salt and pepper.

Place all ingredients except cream in a roomy pan, bring to the boil, level off at simmer, maintain until lentils are quite soft. Fish out rinds, then sieve or emulsify, stir in cream or top of the milk, taste, correct seasoning and optionally, dilute further if considered too thick, with boiling milk.

44 Purée de Celeri-Rave

1 lb washed, scraped celeriac,
boiling water,
2 heaped tablespoonsful flour,
4 pints white bone stock,
2 medium-sized, coarse-grated
old potatoes,

1 oz butter,
salt and pepper,
optional grated cheese to hand
separately.

Mince prepared celeriac. Stir flour to thinish paste with cold water. Pour on a little boiling water, stir into flour, mix thoroughly and then turn into 2 pints boiling water in a pan. Stir until thickened, sink in celeriac, maintain at simmer 1 minute then turn off heat and leave until cool. Strain, rinse clear under running cold water. Reduce stock to 2 pints. Heat butter, fry celeriac gently for 5 minutes, turn into stock. Simmer on very very gently for 35 minutes. Correct seasoning to taste. Serve with fried croûtons (page 17) separately, and optional cheese.

45 Purée Printanier

1 pint basic white sauce
(page 14),
2 oz chopped French beans,
2 oz sliced young carrots,
white and green of 3 spring
onions, chopped,

2 oz baby broad beans in pod,
¼ pint stock or milk,
salt and pepper,
1 bouquet garni.

Heat milk or stock very slowly with herbs. Steam prepared vegetables. When tender mix with half sauce, then sieve, emulsify or liquidise. Return purée to pan, blend in remaining sauce, dilute to required consistency with herb-infused milk or stock (remove herbs first) then season to taste and serve with Pulled Bread (page 12) or *Diablotins* (page 12).

46 Purée de Carottes

*1 pint basic white sauce
   (page 14),
½ lb red of old or whole young
   carrots,
1 sprig fresh or pinch of dried
   chervil,*

*1 heaped dessertspoonful freshly
   milled parsley,
salt and pepper,
extra stock or milk.*

Steam carrots, mash with fork, blend in ¼ pint of sauce then sieve, emulsify or liquidise. Return to pan stir in remaining sauce. Dilute to required consistency with extra chosen fluid, simmer with chervil 7 minutes, taste, correct seasoning, add parsley. Serve with fried croûtons (page 17).

47 Purée de Panais (Parsnip Soup)

*2 pints chicken stock (A or B
   page 125),
1 pint milk,
4 medium parsnips,
1 medium onion,
1 stick celery,*

*1 oz dripping or butter,
1 oz flour,
salt and pepper,
strained juice 1 small lemon.*

Quarter lengthwise, then slice parsnips thinly. Chop onion and celery, slide with parsnips into "singing" butter in frying pan, fry gently without browning, 12 minutes. Scatter flour over and work in with back of wooden spoon. Turn into roomy pan, add stock, simmer 40 minutes, sieve, emulsify or liquidise. Return to pan, stir in milk, simmer 10 minutes. Stir in lemon juice, correct seasoning and serve.

Note: This becomes Crème de Panais if 4 fluid oz thick cream is stirred in at moment of service.

48 Purée St-Germain

1¼ pints shelled fresh peas,
1½ oz butter, or chicken or
  pork fat,
¼ lettuce (preferably Cos), torn
  into minute shreds,
1½ oz green of leeks,
pinch of chervil leaves,
salt and pepper,

1 flat eggspoonful castor sugar,
3 fluid oz stock,
2 pints strong cleared, white
  bone stock (page 124),
1 tablespoonful extra, cooked
  baby peas for scattering over
  servings.

Heat chosen fat, toss in peas, lettuce shreds, chervil leaves, leeks and sugar. Add 3 oz stock and simmer very gently until peas are tender. Sieve or emulsify. Stir in rest of stock, heat to boiling point, stir in butter, correct seasoning and serve with extra peas as garnish.

49 Purée de Laitues 1

2 good-size, well-washed and
  dried Cos lettuces,
2 oz butter,
1 pint milk,
1 gill cream,

salt and pepper,
1 eggspoonful of powdered
  angelica seed or substitute
  lemon thyme, very finely
  chopped.

Dissolve butter in a shallow pan. Poach lettuce carefully until soft. Rub through sieve. Reheat gradually with milk. Correct seasoning, add chosen herb, add cream. If wanting to re-heat do au bain Marie, i.e. in outer pan of hot water.

50 La Soupe des Vendanges (Grape Harvest Soup of the Perigord)

4 pints Bouillon de Boeuf
  (page 129)
1 oz goose or duck fat,
1 oz flour,
2 sticks celery,
2 medium turnips,

½ lb ripe tomatoes,
1 extra oz pork fat,
salt and pepper,
bouquet garni.

Set Pot-au-Feu to simmer in roomy pan. Chop turnips and celery very roughly. Soften goose or duck fat (1 oz), work in flour, cook 3 minutes, work prepared celery and turnips into pot liquor and stir 2 minutes, then leave to simmer. Rough cut tomatoes, add to

fat and flour mixture and stir occasionally until they are totally collapsed. Sieve into Pot-au-Feu mixture, add *bouquet garni*, allow to
simmer on gently for a further 2 hours. Serve strained liquor in
bowls. Hand strained vegetables separately, removing herb bag.

51 Purée de Laitues 2

2 large Cos lettuces,
6 bacon rinds,
1 finely diced rasher of streaky
*   bacon,*
pepper,
1 flat teaspoonful castor sugar,
10 oz peeled, diced old potatoes,

1 oz butter,
1 fluid oz oil,
2 pints very strongly reduced,
*   cleared bone stock (ideally*
*   bacon, ham, gammon or*
*   pork).*

This gives a rare instance of cutting lettuces with a knife. For any
salad item this would spell ruin. Lettuces weep out all their goodness
when so treated; but, since they will be weeping into the soup all
will be well. Wash first, wipe, then shred finely while heating butter
and oil together in a frying pan. Slide in shreds, cook gently until
totally collapsed, turn into a roomy pan, add stock and set over
medium heat. Now fry diced bacon and rinds for 3 minutes at
medium heat, add to pan contents with potatoes and castor sugar,
simmer 30 minutes. Fish out rinds. Sieve or emulsify the rest.
Correct seasoning. Serve with Pulled Bread (page 12).

52 Soup Maigre

1 lb peeled, old potatoes,
1 lb finely chopped onions,
1 herb faggot,
salt and pepper,

2 pints any cleared, strong
*   tasting bone stock,*
1 pint milk,
$\frac{1}{2}$ oz butter,
2 oz stale, grated cheese.

Simmer onions and potatoes in stock with herbs until potatoes
collapse and onions are tender. Remove herbs. Emulsify or sieve,
correct seasoning with salt and pepper, stir in half cheese, add milk
and re-raise to boiling point. Simmer on for 10 minutes. Stir in
butter. Pour into soup bowls, scatter remaining cheese over servings
and hand separate bowl of fried croûtons (page 17).

53 Purée Nesselrode

½ lb nicked, boiled, skinless,
    tender, chestnuts,
2 pints any white meat or bone
    stock, best is chicken,
1 herb faggot,
4 medium onions sliced very
    thinly,

2 oz pork, chicken or ideally
    duck fat,
3 fluid oz dry Madeira,
¼ pint single cream,
1 raw, separated egg yolk,
salt and pepper.

Pound or mill chestnuts finely. Fry onions gently under lid in hot, chosen fat for 15/20 minutes until tender. Place chestnut purée, fried onions, herb faggot and stock in pan. Simmer for 1 hour. Emulsify or sieve, add Madeira, and if deemed too thick dilute with a little extra strongly-reduced white stock. Blend cream and eggs. Turn purée into roomy pan; stand in a meat baking tin half-filled with boiling water and set over a low heat. When piping hot remove, stir in egg/cream mixture beating all the time. Taste, correct seasoning, re-raise to just below boiling point with pan re-set in hot water. Hand fried croûtons (page 17) separately.

54 Purée Crécy

1 lb of the red, outer part of
    large carrots, or all of young
    ones,
1 sprig thyme,
2 oz butter,

1 finely-chopped medium onion,
2 oz rice,
½ pint cleared stock,
1½ pints milk,
salt and pepper.

Scrape carrots, discard old ones' cores, slice finely. Soften butter in a thick pan, add carrots, thyme and onion. Place over low heat and cook very slowly, shaking frequently for 20 minutes. Remove lid, add stock and allow to simmer for 10 minutes. Add milk and rice, stir well and simmer on for a little longer until rice is soft and carrots are tender to taste. Remove thyme, emulsify soup, correct seasoning and serve piping hot.

55 Purée de Tomates

1 oz butter,
lean from 1 bacon rasher,
1 oz red of carrot diced small,
1 shallot or small onion, diced
  small,
8 medium-sized ripe tomatoes,
  rough sliced,

1 generous pinch castor sugar,
2½ oz rice,
1½ pints cleared white bone
  stock,
¼ small bay leaf,
teaspoonful of thyme,
salt and pepper.

Heat butter in a thick pan. Toss in bacon, carrot, onion, thyme and bay leaf and fry gently for 5 minutes; stir in tomatoes, and press them down with a wooden spoon. Add sugar and rice after 4 minutes and stir/turn for 3 minutes more. Pour on stock, bring to the boil. Simmer until rice and carrot are tender, then emulsify or sieve and correct seasoning.

At this stage this simple soup may be served but if you can manage to run 1 oz softened butter through your fingers on to finished soup, then stir in quickly, this considerably enhances the flavour.

Note: This soup may also be made with milk instead of stock.

56 Purée Flamande

1 lb trimmed, steamed until
  tender, Brussels sprouts,
2 medium, peeled potatoes,
  rough-cut,
1 pint white bone stock,

extra milk,
2 fluid oz single cream or
  top-of-milk,
salt and pepper,
1 sprig winter savory.

Add a little of heated stock to rough cut, steamed sprouts and emulsify or sieve. Add potatoes to remaining stock and savory and simmer until potatoes are collapsed. Sieve. Blend with sprout purée. Dilute to required consistency with extra milk, stir in top-of-milk (or single cream), correct seasoning to taste. Hand with small bowl of fried croûtons (page 17) and (optional) bowl of grated hard cheese.

57 Summer Vegetable Soup from the Bearn

7 oz small, peeled turnips,	*1 pint Potage St. Germain*
white of 2 fat leeks,	*(page 57),*
1 lb scraped carrots,	*salt and pepper,*
1 small celery heart,	*1 flat eggspoonful celery salt,*
4½ pints white bone stock,	*3½ oz melted pork fat.*

Dice turnips, carrots and celery; slice leeks thinly. When dissolved pork fat "sings" in frying pan work in vegetables and stir/turn occasionally over low heat until all are collapsed but not browned. Turn into roomy pan, add stock, simmer fairly briskly 40 minutes. Taste, correct seasoning, stir in Potage St. Germain, serve with fried croûtons (page 17).

58 Potage aux Endives

This is Potage Purée de Laitues made with 2 large endive heads instead of lettuce. It can be made with either milk or stock but to explain the curious muddle which the un-initiated get into over the name, what we call Endive the French call *Chicorée*; *Chicorée* (Fr.) is Endive (Eng.). Just to confuse further French *Endive* (Eng. Chicory) is called *Whitloof* in Belgium.

Whatever our chicory is called it remains, we think, **bitter** when cooked. To dispose of bitterness, plunge heads into boiling water with 4 lumps of dissolved sugar. Boil for 3 minutes. Drain, wipe, shred, discard sugar water and use for soup or dressed vegetable item.

59 Potage Maigre

3½ pints strongly reduced bone	*2 finely chopped spring carrots,*
stock,	*4 finely chopped spring onions,*
3 oz alphabetical noodles,	*salt and pepper.*

Place carrots and onions in stock in roomy pan. Simmer until tender, add noodles, simmer 5 minutes. Taste, correct seasoning, serve, handing bowl of grated stale cheese and Hot Garlic Bread (page 13) separately.

60 Potage Sigurd

1½ pints Velouté (page 19),
concentrated tomato purée,
1 flat coffeespoonful chopped,
    fresh mint,
1½ oz grated hard cheese (ideally
    Parmesan),

1 generous pinch cinnamon,
1 flat eggspoonful dry English
    mustard,
1 small Port glass dry sherry
    (cooking type) or dry
    Madeira, either Sercial or
    Verdhelo.

Halve Velouté, turn one half into thick saucepan. Stir in mint and enough tomato purée to make strongly-flavoured tomato sauce. Add to second half the grated cheese, mustard and cinnamon. Beat well. Blend two halves together, raise gently to boiling point and stir for 2 minutes. Stir in Sherry, correct seasoning and serve.

61 Peasant Potage St. Germain

Next time you are compelled to eat what purports to be pea soup at an English hotel, console yourself by returning home to make this excellent brew.

1 pint shelled fresh peas,
2 quarts white bone stock,
2 oz bacon fat, diced small,
1 medium carrot roughly sliced,
1 large rough-chopped onion,
sliced green and white of 1 fat
    leek,

2 rashers lean bacon,
salt and pepper,
1 rounded teaspoonful castor
    sugar,
1 rounded dessertspoonful
    milled parsley heads.

Poach peas in 1 quart of white bone stock, strain peas and set aside. Add a further quart of stock in a large pan and simmer for 1 hour with prepared bacon fat, carrot, onion, leek and diced bacon. Add peas to pan contents and sieve or emulsify. Add stock. Correct seasoning, add sugar and stir in parsley at moment of service.

62 Potage Madelaine

This calls for 3 different purées which are then blended together.

½ lb Jerusalem artichokes,
  steamed, peeled and
  emulsified with ½ pint milk,
½ lb overnight soaked haricot
  beans simmered until tender
  in 1 pint strongly flavoured
  bone stock then emulsified,
½ pint Soubise Sauce (page 17)
  please omit cream,

2 tablespoonsful fine sago,
1 oz butter,
salt and pepper,
extra milk and optional cream,
1 bay leaf,
1 heaped tablespoonful freshly
  milled fresh parsley heads.

Blend together all three purées, add bay leaf and set to simmer gently over low heat and **an asbestos mat**. After 15 minutes sprinkle on sago, stir and simmer on with an occasional stir for 15 minutes, diluting with additional milk if mixture becomes too thick. When desired consistency is obtained correct seasoning, stir in parsley and serve.

Note: Optionally enrich with ¼ pint single cream. Hand grated hard cheese in separate bowl.

63 Potage Potiron Basquaise (Basque Pumpkin and Bean Soup)

10 oz diced pumpkin flesh,
1 walnut butter,
4 oz diced, unsalted pork fat,
4 oz chopped onions,
1/2 crushed garlic cloves,
8 oz overnight-soaked white
  dried beans,

milk,
top-of-milk or single cream,
¼ finely sliced white cabbage,
4 pints chicken stock (A or B
  page 125),
salt and pepper.

Shrivel fat in frying pan, add onions and soft-fry. Scoop into roomy pan with pumpkin, cabbage, beans, crushed garlic, stock and milk. Boil, level off at gentle simmer, maintain under lid 2¼ hours. Taste, correct seasoning, serve with fried croûtons (page 17). Optionally add top-of-milk or cream to taste.

64 Potage Carlton

1½ pints chicken stock (A or B
    page 125),
1½ pints tomato juice,
salt and pepper,
2 oz chicken fat,

2 oz flour,
2 small, coarse-grated shallots
    with their juice,
6 fluid oz single cream,
1 egg.

Blend stock and tomato juice in roomy pan, add shallot pulp and
raise slightly to boiling point. Soften chicken fat in separate pan,
when dissolved remove any shreds of skin and work in the flour
until smooth, soft ball. Add stock mixture gradually, beating well
between each addition. Strain, separate yolk and blend with cream.
At moment of service, with soup at boiling point, pour little into
cream and egg mixture, blend, pour back into pan over asbestos
mat stirring constantly. At final moment, whip egg white stiffly,
turn into soup, whip vigorously, correct seasoning.

65 Potage à la Poissonière

12 shelled shrimps,
2 doz mussels,
2 oz butter,
2 oz flour,
1½ pints milk,
1½ pints fish stock,
1 teaspoonful soft brown sugar,

1 bouquet garni,
1 cod steak (8 oz),
4 sole or plaice fillets from 2
    whole fish,
1 tablespoonful finely chopped
    parsley,
1 gill cream (may be omitted),
¼ pint white wine.

Scrape and beard mussels thoroughly. Place in large pan with sole
carcase left after filleting. Add fish stock, wine, *bouquet garni*, salt
and sugar. Cover and bring to boil over fierce heat. Simmer while
counting 60 slowly. Remove from heat and strain. Pick mussels
from shells and check over lest any scraps of beard remain. Set
aside. Throw shrimps into fish liquor. Set pan back over heat and
count 60 slowly. Strain liquor and add milk. Poach cod steak and
fillets for 6 minutes. Remove both, dice neatly and set aside with
shrimps and mussels. Liquefy butter in clean pan, add flour and
work to smooth ball. Add strained liquor gradually, stirring carefully. Add all fish, fold in cream and parsley.

66 Potage aux Haricots Verts

1 quart good bone stock,
1 lb topped, tailed French or
*   young runner beans,*
salt and pepper,

¼ pint top-of-the-milk or single
*   cream,*
1 sprig thyme or wild thyme
*   (oregano)—optional.*

Place prepared beans in stock with thyme, simmer until tender and then remove thyme and rub through a sieve, emulsify or liquidise. Return to pan, season to taste and serve with diced, fried croûtons (page 17) as a Potage Maigre; or stir in the top-of-the-milk or single cream and serve piping hot with or without a central blob of double cream on each serving.

67 Potage Cultivateur

4 oz chopped red of old carrots,
2 oz chopped turnip,
3 oz chopped white leek,
½ lb chopped shallots or small
*   onions,*
1 fat pinch sugar,
1 fat pinch pepper,
salt,

stock,
6 finely chopped rolled-up
*   leaves of stemless spinach,*
4 oz coarse-grated raw potato,
2 oz diced, raw, unsalted pork
*   fat,*
1 herb faggot,
1 oz dripping.

Put pork dice and dripping in thick frying pan. When "singing", add carrots, turnip, leek and shallots and fry over moderate heat for 5 minutes. Scrape into pan, cover liberally with stock, immerse herb faggot and simmer for 1 hour. Slide in raw, grated potato. Cook for further 15 minutes. Slide in shredded spinach and allow 3 minutes more. Fish out herbs, season and serve with or without Pulled Bread (page 12), fried croûtons (page 17) and/or grated stale cheese.

Veloutés

68. Velouté Cressonière
69. Velouté de Chou-Fleur d'Italie
70. Red Bean Soup
71. Velouté aux Haricots Verts
72. Velouté d'Epinards
73. Velouté Chivry
74. Velouté de Concombres
75. Velouté Dame-Blanche
76. Velouté au Pourpier
77. Velouté aux Topinambours
78. Velouté Rosé
79. White Bean Soup

68 Velouté Cressonière

4 standard bunches fresh
   watercress,
1¼ pints thin Velouté (page 19),

salt and pepper,
1 generous eggspoonful celery
   salt,
boiling water.

Pick over and wash watercress very thoroughly. Place in pan, pour boiling water over, leave 5 minutes, drain and return to pan. Add Velouté. Re-raise to boiling point over low heat stirring carefully, then simmer gently for 8 minutes not forgetting an occasional stir lest it catch on base of pan. Emulsify, correct seasoning and serve.

Alternative accompaniments: Diced, fried croûtons (page 17), grated cheese or ¼ inch rounds from a very narrow "flute" of French bread, toasted and spread with Garlic Butter (page 18).

69 Velouté de Chou-fleur d'Italie

½ pint basic white sauce
   (page 14),
1½ pints cleared, well-reduced
   bone stock,
½ lb steamed broccoli spears,

salt and pepper,
1 sprig winter savory,
½ oz butter.

Chop steamed broccoli. Mix with ¼ pint stock, sieve, emulsify or liquidise. Turn into roomy pan. Stir in remaining stock, white sauce, finely chopped savory, simmer 5 minutes. Taste, correct seasoning, stir in butter in small flakes.

70 Red Bean Soup

Please turn to White Bean Soup (page 66). Copy exactly using 1 lb of red beans instead of white and replacing a claret type "plonk" wine with a Burgundy type.

71 Velouté aux Haricots Verts

It is naughty to use the reed slim beans for this soup as we should always do when employing them as vegetables. Gardeners will know that some grow on beyond reed-slender to middle-aged-spread through having been missed by pickers! Use these for soup. Top and tail, checking that they have not become stringy. If they have, then remove side strands; chop up beans and they are ready to use.

1 lb chopped, prepared French beans,
1½ pints Velouté (page 19),

6 little spring onions (whites only),
salt and pepper.

Steam both beans and white of onions until both are tender. Take ½ pint Velouté and blend in both cooked vegetables. Emulsify or sieve, add remaining Velouté, correct seasoning and serve, or dilute to desired consistency with extra milk.

Note: Milled parsley or chives in a side dish for sprinkling over will further enhance this soup.

72 Velouté d'Epinards (Spinach Soup)

1½ oz flour,
1½ oz butter,
1 generous oz grated hard cheese,

1 generous pinch nutmeg,
salt and pepper,
1 pint milk,
6 oz cooked, sieved spinach.

Dissolve butter in roomy pan, add flour, stir until mixture forms soft ball, add milk and spinach gradually, beating well between each addition. Season with nutmeg, salt and pepper to taste. When all liquid is absorbed add cheese. If desired, soup can be advance-made for re-heating in double pan over hot water later. When feeling extravagant pour cream into top centre of each filled bowl. If soup is considered too thick, thin down further with milk.

73 Velouté Chivry

1 pint Velouté, (page 19),
3 pints duck stock, follow
  chicken stock, (page 125),
1 coffeespoonful each of chervil
  leaves, chopped tarragon,
  milled parsley heads and
  2 of chives,

(when possible add 1 eggspoonful chopped pimpernel—must
  be young otherwise it is
  bitter),
3 oz diced cooked duck flesh,
1 oz butter,
¼ pint whipping cream.

Simmer duck stock with all herbs until reduced to 1 pint. Blend with Velouté and simmer on for 5 minutes. Taste, correct seasoning.
  Run in softened butter through fingers, stir and finally stir in whipping cream and diced duck flesh.

74 Velouté de Concombres

1 large cucumber coarsely
  grated,
salt and pepper,
1 eggspoonful castor sugar,

1 pint Velouté (page 19),
1 pint chicken stock A or B
  (page 125),
¼ pint top-of-milk or cream.

Place cucumber in pan with stock and simmer for 20 minutes. Sieve or emulsify; return to pan, stir in Velouté, sugar, top-of-milk or cream and correct seasoning.

75 Velouté Dame-Blanche

1½ oz chicken or duck fat or
  butter,
1½ oz flour,
1½ pints clear chicken stock A
  or B (page 125),
12 sweet, blanched almonds,

4 oz finely chopped, cooked,
  white chicken meat,
1 dessertspoonful freshly milled
  parsley heads,
salt and pepper.

Soften the chosen fat in a thick pan, work in the flour and stir to soft ball over a low heat. Dilute gradually with chicken stock beating absolutely smooth after each addition. Put the almonds through a cheese mill or chop finely, then pound down to a paste. Stir into soup, taste, correct seasoning. Mix parsley with chicken dice. Sprinkle some over each bowlful.

76 Velouté au Pourpier

This is made with purslane which Culpeper called "herb of the moon". Purslane is half-hardy, can be grown on the herb bed and can provide an aromatic and very acceptable soup. Turn to page 62 and follow exactly the instructions for Velouté Cressonière. Use four bunches of purslane picked to approximate four standard bunches of shop-bought watercress.

77 Velouté aux Topinambours

We are always saddened by the neglect of this excellent winter vegetable which grows like big sunflowers, providing a splendid kitchen garden border wind-break. Stems are cut down in late autumn. Artichokes remain available throughout the winter months for use in vegetarian main-course dishes, raw and grated in salads (when it tastes like Brazil nuts!) and in soups.

1½ lb steamed, scrubbed, unpeeled Jerusalem artichokes,	1 oz grated stale cheese, 1 generous pinch nutmeg, salt and pepper,
2 pints Velouté (page 19),	extra milk.

Peel steamed artichokes (knobbles are much easier to contend with after steaming). Slice rapidly into Velouté, emulsify, dilute if considered too thick with extra milk, correct seasoning, add nutmeg and hand more grated cheese separately.

Note: When steaming the artichokes for the first time, allow time for testing. For emulsifying into soup they should be **very** tender, but **not** for when serving as a vegetable. Set the two times for yourselves. Then a pinger or ringer can take care of the job while you do something else!

78 Velouté Rosé

(Pink Soup, much used at Victorian/Edwardian Pink Luncheons when all food, cloths, napkins, flowers and china were pink!)

2½ pints milk,
1 rounded tablespoonful potato
    flour or Arrowroot,
2 rounded tablespoonsful
    concentrated tomato purée,
1 separated egg yolk,

2 fluid oz double cream,
salt and pepper,
1 heaped tablespoonful scissored
    chives (see Frozen Chives
    page 15),
1 flat teaspoonful paprika.

Mix tomato purée, paprika and arrowroot or potato flour in bowl. Work down to smooth paste with a little of given milk. Bring remainder of milk to boil, pour some on to bowl mix, stir well, pour back into pan and stir over moderate heat 5 minutes. Blend egg yolk with cream, pour on a little hot soup, return to pan off heat, stir fast, taste, correct seasoning and stir in chives.

79 White Bean Soup

1 lb white beans,
4 pints cold water,
½ oz real salt,
1 large onion stuck with 2
    cloves,
1 lengthwise quartered carrot,
1 bouquet garni,

¾ oz diced, unsalted pork fat
    (try for one slightly streaked
    with meat),
8 fluid oz rough, red wine
    (plonk!),
pepper and salt.

Soak beans for 24 hours in cold water. Wash well, place in casserole with all remaining ingredients except seasonings. Bring to the boil over moderate heat, cover, put into low oven one shelf below centre. Cook until beans are tender. Then sieve or emulsify, removing cloves from onion. In French style this soup will almost prop up a spoon it is so thick. Fried croûtons (page 17) are added to make it even more solid; but if dilution is required, try to do so with strong giblet stock which imparts a distinctive flavour to the finished soup.

Iced Soups

80 Health Soup No. 1 (no cooking)

$\frac{1}{2}$ lb spinach with stalks removed,
6 oz chopped white of celery,
4 oz finely grated raw carrot,

salt, pepper and celery salt,
2 standard cartons plain
   yoghurt,
milk.

Place prepared spinach in liquidiser or emulsifier and switch to full. Maintain until mixture is creamy. Sieve into a roomy bowl. Stir in chopped celery and grated carrot, blend in yoghurt, season to taste. Stir in milk to obtain desired consistency. Refrigerate. Serve with 2 ice cubes in each bowl and an optional top sprinkling of milled, fresh parsley heads.

81 Health Soup No. 2 (no cooking)

1 bunch carefully picked,
   trimmed, washed watercress,
1 pint tinned tomato juice,
1 rounded teaspoonful celery
   salt,

3/4 drops Worcestershire
   sauce,
salt and pepper,
$\frac{1}{2}$ pint cold, cleared stock.

Emulsify or liquidise watercress with part of tomato juice. Tip into roomy bowl. Add all remaining ingredients. Season to taste, chill in refrigerator until required. Pour over 2 ice cubes dropped into each bowl.

82 Health Soup No. 3 (no cooking)

$\frac{1}{4}$ lb grated, cooked beetroot,
$\frac{1}{4}$ lb white of celery chopped
   small and liquidised or
   emulsified with 8 fluid oz
   cold, clear stock,

6 fat heads of parsley with
   stems on liquidised or
   emulsified with 8 fluid oz
   stock,
1 carton soured cream,
salt and pepper.

Blend prepared beetroot with celery liquid, parsley liquid and soured cream. Season to taste, refrigerate until required. Pour over bowls containing 2 ice cubes. Optionally sprinkle tops of servings with finely scissored fresh or thawed, frozen chives.

83 Health Soup No. 4 (no cooking)

1 heart of lettuce (Cos or
  cabbage),
1 oz raw white cabbage,
one 5 inch stick white of celery,
one 2 inch chunk unpeeled,
  chopped cucumber,
1 small peeled crushed garlic
  clove,
1 sprig picked watercress,

½ medium green pimento,
  de-pithed and seeded,
1 large ripe tomato, rough-cut
  after skinning,
salt and pepper,
1 teaspoonful celery salt,
strained juice of 1 orange and
  of ½ lemon,
1 pint tinned tomato juice,
½ pint water.

Shred lettuce, put with cabbage and chopped celery into emulsifyer or liquidiser with half given water. Switch on fully until thoroughly pulped. Tip into roomy bowl and repeat with cucumber, garlic clove, watercress and remaining water. When in pulp, add to first mixture and repeat with tomato, pimento and ¼ pint of tomato juice. When all three pulps are blended add remaining tomato juice, orange juice, celery salt, lemon juice, stir very thoroughly, taste and correct seasoning. Chill and serve with 2 ice cubes to each bowl.

84 Chlodnik (Iced Balkan Soup)

½ lb well-washed beetroot leaves,
1 lb small well-scrubbed
  beetroots,
3 oz shelled brown or pink
  shrimps, chopped
1 chopped hard-boiled egg,
4½ pints slightly salted water,

½ small cucumber grated
  un-skinned,
1 large sprig dill or fennel,
1 rounded tablespoonful finely
  scissored chives,
4 fluid oz beer,
salt and pepper,
1 carton soured cream.

Place beetroots and leaves in salted water, simmer until tender. Drain liquor into clean pan. Rough-cut beetroots, fork down thoroughly. Chop leaves finely. Return all to salted water. Add remaining ingredients except 2 oz shrimps and chives. Taste, correct seasonings, sieve soup, chill and serve icily chilled with 1/2 ice cubes in each serving; sprinkle tops with chives and remaining shrimps.

85 Crème des Haricots Verts Glacée

1 lb slim young French beans,
3 pints strongly-reduced clear
   stock,
1 garlic clove (peeled),

1 sprig thyme,
7 fluid oz single cream,
salt and pepper,
ice cubes.

Top, tail and rough chop French beans. Place in stock with thyme
and garlic. Simmer until beans are tender. Remove sprig, liquidise,
then simmer down to 2 pints. Stir in cream, taste, correct seasonings,
serve icily chilled with 1/2 ice cubes in each serving.

86 Iced Vinaigrette Soup

$\frac{1}{4}$ pint well-shaken Vinaigrette,
1 pint well reduced chicken stock
   (A page 125),
strained juice of 1 lemon,
3 fluid oz boiling water,
1 oz fine dice of unskinned
   tomato,

2 oz de-pipped and pithed green
   or red pimento,
2 inches of unskinned cucumber,
2 oz brown crumbs,
fried croûtons (page 17),
ice cubes and 1 heaped
   teaspoonful concentrated
   tomato purée.

Turn Vinaigrette into wooden bowl. Stir in boiling water, then cold
stock, tomato purée and lemon juice. Add diced vegetables. At
moment of service divide crumbs between 4 soup plates. Add one
ice cube apiece and pour in soup. Hand croûtons separately for
spoonsful to be stirred in.

Vinaigrette. Put flat teaspoonful salt, $\frac{1}{2}$ flat teaspoonful pepper, 1
flat eggspoonful French mustard in wooden bowl and beat with
drips of oil totalling $\frac{1}{2}$ pint, and alternate drips wine vinegar
totalling 1 fluid oz. Blend in 1 oz mixed finely chopped tarragon,
chives, parsley heads and chervil. Bottle and store indefinitely in
cool place NOT refrigerator.

87 Iced Zucchini and Corn Soup

2 heads fresh corn,
1 shallot or small onion,
1 crushed garlic clove,
1 fluid oz oil,
1 pint beef bone stock (well
  reduced),

1 pint well-reduced white bone
  stock,
5 fluid oz single cream,
2 zucchini or courgettes,
salt and white pepper.

Heat oil. When "singing" fry finely chopped shallot or onion and garlic until very soft, add both stocks. Immerse whole corn cobs and simmer under lid gently until tender. Lift out, drain and cut away all kernels. Return these to pan, simmer 5 minutes more with thinly sliced unpeeled zucchini or courgettes. Chill, stir in cream, taste, correct seasoning, serve icily chilled.

88 Gazpacho

2 lb small, ripe tomatoes,
2 large Spanish onions,
salt, pepper and celery salt,
2 peeled crushed garlic cloves,
6 raw bacon rinds,
$\frac{1}{4}$ lb green pimentoes,
$\frac{1}{4}$ lb yellow pimentoes,

1 medium-sized hot-house
  cucumber,
$\frac{1}{4}$ white crustless loaf,
$1\frac{1}{2}$ gills cooking sherry,
2 dessertspoonsful tarragon
  vinegar,
4 large firm tomatoes,
2 fluid oz olive oil.

Halve small tomatoes and slice onions. Place both with garlic and bacon rinds in large pan. Cover generously with water, add oil, bring to the boil, simmer gently for 1 hour, remove rinds, then sieve. Add sherry and vinegar. Correct seasoning and chill very thoroughly.
  Serve in soup-bowls and hand four separate side dishes:
  1. the cucumber, skinned and neatly diced;
  2. the 4 large tomatoes, skinned, seeded and neatly diced;
  3. the pimentoes, with all the pips and white rinds carefully removed, and neatly diced;
  4. bread, neatly diced and browned very slowly in the oven at 290 F (gas 1) middle shelf.
  Each guest takes a generous spoonful from each of the side dishes and stirs all together into the very cold soup.

89 Iced Malaga Soup (Spanish—no cooking)

1 red (or green) pimento,
½ unskinned cucumber,
2 standard cartons yoghurt,
2 oz peeled de-pipped, ripe
  tomato flesh (you can use
  tinned for this),
½ pint strained orange juice
  (substitute tinned, un-
  sweetened if necessary),
celery salt,
salt and pepper,
1 standard carton soured cream.

De-pith, de-pip and dice the chosen pimento small. Coarse-grate the unskinned cucumber conserving every scrap of juice. Rub chosen tomato pulp through an ordinary sieve and toss all into a roomy bowl. Blend in the yoghurt, orange juice and soured cream, correct seasoning with given flavours and refrigerate until 20 minutes before service. Then add 8 ice cubes, stir well and serve.

90 Iced Young Garden Peas and Mint Soup (no cooking)

¾ lb steamed, cold, young peas,
1 carton yoghurt,
½ carton soured cream,
1 pint milk,
1½ oz cooked lean ham or
  gammon,
6 ice cubes,
3 small mint heads, chopped
  finely,
salt and pepper.

Mix everything except seasoning and ice and emulsify or liquidise and then season to taste. Pour over ice cubes into a jug and re-frigerate until service. Optionally, scatter with finely-scissored chives.

91 Iced Shrimp and Orange Soup (no cooking)

4 oz shelled shrimps,
6 fluid oz strained orange juice,
1 standard small carton yoghurt,
1 standard carton soured
  cream,
strained juice of ½ small lemon,
black pepper,
1 small bunch carefully-picked
  watercress,
12 ice cubes.

Set aside 6 fat little watercress heads, pick leaves from rest, put these leaves with all ingredients except pepper, ice and shrimps, into emulsifier or liquidiser, switch on fully and stop when all is perfectly blended. Fold in 3 oz chopped shrimps. Stir, taste, add pepper only. Pour into jug over 6 ice cubes. Refrigerate until moment of service. Pour into 6 soup bowls, add extra ice cube to each, float a few of remaining shrimps on top and tuck a watercress sprig into one side of each bowl.

92 Piquant Iced Tomato Soup (no cooking)

10 fluid oz tinned tomato juice,
10 fluid oz well-reduced cleared
  bone stock,
1 rounded teaspoonful powdered
  celery salt,
½ crushed garlic clove,

8 ice cubes,
¼ a standard bunch watercress,
6 stem-denuded large spinach
  leaves,
4 finely-chopped mint heads.

Stir tinned tomato juice in with bone stock. Add powdered celery salt, garlic clove and 8 ice cubes. Put carefully-washed watercress into emulsifier or liquidiser with 2 fluid oz of the blended fluids and spinach leaves. Switch on and when a smooth purée is achieved, stir into the rest of the mixture. Refrigerate in a jug with 4 more ice cubes. At moment of service, sprinkle each bowlful with finely-chopped mint heads and add one ice cube to each bowl.

93 Iced Black Cherry and Celery Soup (no cooking)

1 carton plain yoghurt,
¼ carton soured cream,
¾ pint chicken stock,
½ lb stoned black cherries and
  juice,

1 white celery head,
pinch each of salt and castor
  sugar,
2 finely-chopped mint leaves,
black pepper to taste.

Chop, then emulsify or liquidise celery with stock. Add all remaining ingredients, stir well, refrigerate, place two ice cubes in each bowl before pouring on soup.

94 Quick, Iced Cucumber Soup (no cooking)

1 large peeled cucumber,
2 rough-cut peeled tomatoes,
4 fluid oz dryish white cooking
* wine,*
1 pint best milk,
¼ pint double cream,

1 heaped teaspoonful freshly
* milled parsley,*
1 heaped dessertspoonful
* scissored chives,*
salt and pepper.

Coarse-grate cucumber, emulsify or liquidise with wine, then scoop with juice left from grating into pan. Add all remaining ingredients, correct seasoning, chill and pour over 1 ice cube in each chosen bowl.

95 Iced Beetroot Soup

1 lb coarse-grated, peeled,
* cooked beetroot,*
1½ pints very strongly reduced
* beef stock,*
1 rounded tablespoonful freshly
* milled parsley heads,*
1 flat eggspoonful powdered
* bay leaf,*

1 rounded teaspoonful celery
* salt,*
1 (optional) totally pulped
* garlic clove,*
1 dessertspoonful juice from a
* raw, grated onion,*
salt and pepper,
2 oz stiffly whipped cream,
8 ice cubes.

Set aside 1 heaped tablespoonful of grated beetroot. Turn remainder into cold stock, add onion juice, bay and parsley; emulsify, taste, correct seasoning, and refrigerate. For service mix whipped cream with remaining beetroot. Put 2 ice cubes into each serving bowl. Pour on soup and put a blob of cream mixture centrally upon each.

flesh of 1 ripe, halved avocado
  with stone removed,
1 carton soured cream,
4 chopped walnut halves,
1 chopped hard boiled egg,
½ pint bottled, unsweetened
  apple juice,

1 tiny head of mint chopped
  finely,
1 pinch salt,
white pepper,
strained juice of ½ lemon.

Mix all, save mint, slicing avocado roughly with silver knife to prevent blackening. Emulsify or liquidise, turn into a jug, refrigerate. Stir in mint and 6 ice cubes 30 minutes before service. If deemed too thick, dilute with White Bone Stock (page 124) or Chicken Stock A or B (page 125).

97 Iced Avocado and Crab Meat Soup (no cooking)

3 oz brown crab meat,
1 ripe avocado,
1 small carton of plain yoghurt,
½ small carton soured cream,
salt and black pepper,

¾ pint cold, white bone or
  chicken stock,
strained juice of ½ small lemon,
same quantity of water,
12 ice cubes,
1 rounded tablespoonful milled,
  fresh parsley heads.

Peel avocado with silver knife to prevent blackening, turn into small bowl, mix lemon juice and water, pour over, turn well, refrigerate. Put crab meat, yoghurt, cream and stock into emulsifier, liquidiser or just sieve. Switch on full. Stop when absolutely blended. Pour into jug over 6 ice cubes. Correct seasoning. Drain avocado pieces, mash and stir into soup. At moment of service divide between six chosen bowls, adding 1 ice cube to each and sprinkling parsley overall.

98 Iced Pineapple and Cream Cheese Soup

one 1 inch thick strip fresh
pineapple, emulsified,
liquidised or sieved,
1 standard carton plain yoghurt,
¼ carton soured cream,
2 oz cream cheese,

salt and pepper,
1 oz grated unskinned cucumber
with juices,
½ pint milk,
1 heaped tablespoonful scissored
chives,
ice cubes.

Emulsify all ingredients except treated pineapple, seasonings and ice. When smooth and creamy season and refrigerate. At moment of service, stir in pineapple, taste, correct seasoning, pour over 1/2 ice cubes in each glass or cup. Scatter chives overall.

99 Iced Georgia Soup (no cooking)

2 de-pipped, peeled tomatoes,
1 de-pithed and pipped pimento,
1 large Spanish onion,
1 crushed garlic clove,
red of 1 large carrot,
1 oz mixed, freshly milled
parsley, tarragon, basil and
chives,
3 fluid oz olive oil,
1 tablespoonful wine vinegar,

1 dessertspoonful lemon juice,
1 bunch watercress,
3 pints chicken stock B
(page 125),
10 oz peeled, diced cucumber,
¼ teaspoonful celery salt,
salt and pepper,
1 scant flat teaspoonful paprika
powder,
dash of real, Worcestershire
sauce

Finely chop tomato flesh and pimento. Grate onion, carrot and cucumber finely. Mix with picked, chopped watercress leaves and small heads. Put celery salt, ½ flat teaspoonful salt, 3 drops Worcestershire sauce, paprika, garlic and 2 generous pinches pepper into wooden bowl. Work up with oil, lemon and drips of vinegar, turn on to vegetables. Taste and correct final seasoning. Stir in chilled, cleared stock, cover with clean cloth and refrigerate minimum 5 hours. Serve icily chilled with Garlic Bread (page 13).

100 Bortsch (Russian Beetroot Soup)

1 large or 2 small coarsely
    grated raw beetroots,
1 large or 2 small coarsely
    grated raw onions,
2 sticks white celery,
½ of the green and all of white
    of 1 leek,
2 large cabbage leaves,
1 very small crushed garlic
    clove,
2 peppercorns,
1 pinch cayenne,

1 tablespoonful red wine vinegar,
1 flat dessertspoonful soft brown
    sugar,
3 pints stock,
3 oz butter,
3 fluid oz oil,
1 large, skinned, chopped,
    de-pipped tomato,
bouquet garni,
salt and pepper,
1 small carton soured cream.

Cover beetroot with vinegar. Chop celery, leek and cabbage finely. Heat butter and oil together in sauté or frying pan. Soft fry onion, leek, celery and beetroot, covered, for 8 minutes over low heat. Turn into saucepan, add remaining ingredients except cream with seasonings. Boil, skim and simmer for 2 hours. Strain and serve hot with 1 tablespoonful soured cream slid on top of each bowlful. Or serve cold (when it sets like jelly) forked up into a froth with blobs of soured cream on top.

101 Emergency Iced Celery Soup

1 large tin celery hearts,
1¼ pints milk,
¼ pint top-of-milk or single
    cream,

1 generously heaped dessert-
    spoonful scissored chives,
2 oz grated hard cheese,
salt and pepper.

Place celery hearts, their fluid and ¼ pint milk in emulsifier or liquidiser. Switch on until pulped. Rub through sieve, mix in all remaining ingredients except cheese, taste, correct seasoning; chill in refrigeration until required. Pour over 1/2 ice cubes into bowls. Scatter hard, grated cheese overall.

Frozen Soups (introduction)

We have discovered a nice range of real soups which can be puréed then frozen. When thawed, the purées are heated and diluted for service. The purées can be frozen in polythene bags with closures, but these attain rather messy shapes so we recommend the use of small square or rectangular lidded plastic boxes which stack neatly and can be labelled easily.

102 Frozen Cucumber Soup

2 cucumbers,
1¼ pints very strongly reduced
  bone stock,

1 pint milk,
¼ pint single or coffee cream,
salt.

Slice cucumbers paper thin with skins left on. Place in pan with stock and simmer with extreme gentleness until cucumbers are very soft. Emulsify or liquidise. Turn into waxed carton and freeze. When required, thaw carton overnight. Turn puree into a roomy pan. Stir in milk then cream, taste, correct seasoning, turn into a tureen, add 6 ice cubes and leave for up to 4 hours before serving.

103 Frozen Vichyssoise

Please turn to recipe on page 151. Follow this through the cooking of the leeks and potatoes in strong stock. Emulsify. Freeze. Thaw when required. Heat over low flame, stir in milk to taste, correct seasoning, "finish" with top-of-milk or single cream. Serve with fresh, scissored or thawed, frozen chives in separate bowls.

104 Frozen Potage St. Germain

Follow the recipe on page 57 as far as the purée completion. Pack into lidded, small, plastic boxes and freeze. When required, thaw out and complete soup as given on page 57 for Potage St. Germain.

Meat and Poultry Soups

105. Chicken and Banana Soup
106. Lord Mayor's Soup
107. Cock-a-Leekie
108. Hotch-Potch
109. Mulligatawny
110. Boiled Brisket Left-Overs Soup
111. Oxtail Soup
112. Rabbit Soup
113. Filling Oxtail Soup
114. Vermicelli Soep Met Ballettes
115. Creole Pepper Pot
116. Boxing Night Soup
117. Easter Soup
118. Tschi
119. Mock Turtle Soup
120 Potage des Abatis de Volaille
121. Ham or Gammon Bone and Pea Soup
122. Scotch Broth
123. Kidney Soup

105 Chicken and Banana Soup (American)

2½ pints chicken stock A or B   4 small ripe bananas,
  (page 125),   ¼ pint top-of-the-milk,
¼ pint single cream,   salt and pepper, cinnamon.

Mix milk, cream and stock in roomy pan. Simmer 5 minutes. Mash and then emulsify bananas with ¼ pint of cooled liquid. Stir into pan, taste, season with pinch or two of salt and plenty of pepper, pour into bowls. Sprinkle powdered cinnamon lightly over servings.

106 Lord Mayor's Soup

2 lb veal bones,   salt and pepper,
1 medium onion,   2 oz dripping,
1 medium carrot,   2 unsalted raw pig's trotters,
2 outside sticks celery,   1 boiling fowl,
1 trimmed leek,   8 pints beef bone stock,
4 parsley stalks,   1 bouquet garni.

Heat dripping in meat baking tin. Put in bones, whole carrot, onion, celery sticks, leek and parsley stalks and roast in oven, mid-shelf at 355 F (gas 4) turning after 10 minutes, for overall 20 minutes. Drain off any residue fat, place in large pot with pig's trotters and fowl smashed down to a pulp, *bouquet garni* and stock. Bring to boil, skim, simmer 2½ hours quite gently. Excavate trotters. Cut removed skin into small squares, place in lightly salted boiling water, simmer until almost transparent, strain. Strain off pot liquor, skim as for beef bone stock (page 4), return to pot, add diced carrot, finely sliced rounds of leek, white and green, correct seasoning and simmer fairly strongly for 30 minutes, to reduce.

For service A: merely add 6 fluid oz dry, cooking-type sherry.

For service B: if preferred, soup may be thickened with 1 oz potato flour or arrowroot dissolved in a little cold water. Stir in and serve.

107 Cock-A-Leekie

*5 pints strongly reduced white
  bone stock,
1 small boiling fowl,
8 slim or 4 fat leeks,
1 bouquet garni,*

*4 oz overnight soaked pearl
  barley,
salt and pepper,
2 oz dripping.*

Divide fowl into small, neat pieces. Heat fat, when "singing" fry fowl on both sides, lift into roomy pan, add stock, bring to boil, skim, steady off at simmer. Slice white and green of leeks thinly. After 1 hour, add, with herbs to stock, simmer for further 1 hour. Skim off top fat with absorbent kitchen paper, add barley, simmer on until barley is tender, strain, fish out purged chicken carcase. Cut 4–6 oz flesh into dice, add to soup, taste, correct seasoning and serve.

108 Hotch-Potch

*2 quarts strong bone stock,
1½ lb neck mutton,
1 large Spanish onion,
1 large quartered carrot,
¼ large turnip,
½ pint shelled peas,*

*1 Cos lettuce,
1 rounded dessertspoonful
  freshly milled parsley,
salt and pepper,
1 bouquet garni.*

Rough-cut neck meat, place in roomy pan with stock, boil, skim, steady off at simmer. Dice all vegetables except peas. After 1 hour, add to pan with herbs, simmer on 30 minutes. Add peas, simmer further 30 minutes, taste, correct seasoning, strain, excavate neck meat, cut into dice, stir in. Stir in parsley and serve.

109 Mulligatawny

2 quarts mutton bone stock,
1 lb neck of mutton,
2 medium onions,
2 medium carrots,
2 medium cooking apples,
1 small turnip,
1 bouquet garni,

1 oz flour,
1 mean flat dessertspoonful
  Masala paste,
strained juice ½ lemon,
pinch cayenne,
salt.

Trim mutton free of all fat. Dissolve fat in shallow pan, remove residue, dice all vegetables and fry in fat gently, turning occasionally, for 12 minutes. Scatter flour over surface, work in with back of wooden spoon, add and work in Masala paste. Turn into pot, add mutton, herbs and liquor, stir until mixture boils, steady off at simmer, cook gently under lid 2 hours. Strain, place meat with ¼ pint liquor in emulsifier or liquidiser and reduce to pulp or sieve. Return to pot. Add lemon juice and cayenne, season to taste, hand cooked Patna rice in bowl, separately.

110 Boiled Brisket Left-Overs Soup

This is more a suggestion than a recipe but it **is** delicious! When you have boiled and served a boned, rolled, salted brisket of beef with potatoes, onions and carrots, there is almost invariably (if properly cooked) a remainder of vegetables, at least 1 slice of meat and about 1½ pints of liquor left. Put all into a roomy pan, then with a well-scrubbed hand, and when liquor is warm, crush vegetables up small, bring to boiling point and add either Semolina Dumplings (page 19) or Liver Dumplings (page 20). Poach on gently until dumplings rise. Serve as a meal-in-itself-soup.

111 Oxtail Soup

1 small, jointed oxtail,
1 quart beef stock,
2 onions,
2 carrots,
1 turnip,
2 sticks celery,
2 oz dripping,
2 oz lean, raw bacon,

1 bouquet garni,
4 peppercorns,
salt and pepper,
seasoned flour (page 18),
3 fluid oz cooking-type sherry,
optional few drops
   Worcestershire sauce.

Divide tail at joints, turn in seasoned flour, heat dripping. When "singing" fry bacon dice and oxtail briskly, turn until browned all over. Place in roomy pot, cover with stock, add herbs, peppercorns and diced vegetables, bring to boil, skim and simmer gently under lid for 3 hours minimum, or until oxtail falls from bones. Remove top fat with absorbent kitchen paper. Remove meat and bones. Separate flesh into small pieces. Reboil liquor, return meat to pan, stir, taste, correct seasoning, remove bouquet garni, stir in sherry and serve.

Note: When making Oxtail main course for freezing we use 2/3 of the narrow tail ends for soup and casserole the rest.

112 Rabbit Soup

1 small rabbit,
3 pints white bone stock,
3 oz diced gammon or lean
   bacon,
1 stick celery, chopped,
1 medium onion, chopped

1 bouquet garni,
2 oz butter or dripping,
salt and pepper,
seasoned flour (page 18),
$\frac{1}{2}$ pint milk,
optional $\frac{1}{4}$ pint single cream.

Joint rabbit pieces neatly. Turn in seasoned flour. Heat chosen fat until "singing", fry pieces briskly until brown. Place in roomy pan, with stock, bacon or gammon, onion, celery and herbs. Boil, skim, simmer 1½ hours. Excavate rabbit pieces and herbs. Cut meat from saddle pieces, dice, return to pan, add milk, re-boil and simmer 20 minutes. Stir in optional cream, correct seasoning, serve with fried croûtons (page 17).

113 Filling Oxtail Soup

*1 small, jointed oxtail divided
  into neat pieces,
seasoned flour,
2 oz clean dripping,
1 herb faggot,
washed, chopped, outer stems
  of a celery head,*

*1 large, sliced Spanish onion,
2 lengthwise split, then chopped
  carrots,
2 quarts beef-bone stock,
2 oz pearl barley,
cayenne pepper.*

Dissolve and heat dripping in large frying pan. Pass oxtail pieces
through seasoned flour. When dripping "sings", fry oxtail briskly
until well-browned. Lift out, fry onion in residue over lower heat
turning the while for a maximum 5 minutes. Place in a large saucepan with oxtail, herbs, prepared vegetables, barley and stock. Bring
to the boil, skim thoroughly, refresh with 5 fluid oz cold water, re-
boil, level off at a steady simmer and maintain until flesh falls away
from oxtail bones.

Fish out oxtail, simmer remaining pan contents to reduce to 2½
pints. Break up meat into neat pieces. Return to pan, taste, correct
seasoning, remove herb bag and add a single generous pinch of
cayenne. Optionally finish with a squeeze of lemon juice. Leave
until cold. Lift off all top-crusted, set, fat. Reheat for service.

Note: A small port-glass of sherry may be added to this soup. Also,
when suitable to baking pattern and to conserve fuel this soup may
be cooked in a lidded casserole on lower part of a slow oven. Cooking continues until flesh falls from oxtail pieces and carrots are
tender.

114 Vermicelli Soep met Ballettes (Dutch Vermicelli Soup with Meat Balls)

*1 quart any bone stock,
2 blades mace,
4 oz minced raw lamb, beef,
  mutton, pork or any liver,
salt and pepper,*

*grated nutmeg,
flour,
2 oz fine crushed vermicelli,
1 rounded dessertspoonful
  freshly milled parsley heads.*

Place mace and stock in roomy pan, bring to boil, simmer gently
15 minutes. Meanwhile put chosen meat or liver into bowl, season

with salt, pepper and nutmeg, shape into marble-sized balls, roll in flour. Remove mace blades. Scatter vermicelli over soup, slide in meat balls, cover pan, simmer gently 20 minutes. Sprinkle parsley heads over each serving.

115 Creole Pepper Pot

1 lb single tripe,
1 lb honeycomb or double tripe,
2 medium potatoes,
2 parsley stalks,
1 veal knuckle bone,
3 quarts water,

1 bouquet garni,
1 medium onion, chopped,
cayenne,
salt and pepper,
$\frac{1}{2}$ one small lengthwise split hot red pepper.

Place knuckle in roomy pot or pan. Cover with given water, boil, skim, add herb bag, parsley stalks and red pepper, simmer 3 hours. Cut both tripes into finger strips, add to knuckle, simmer on very gently with onion, herbs and red pepper until tripe is absolutely tender. After 1 hour add rough-diced potatoes. Remove knuckle, remove any meatscraps, cut these small, return to soup. When boiling, taste, correct seasoning, fish out herb bag, parsley stalks and pepper, serve.

116 Boxing Night Soup

the strained, cleared liquor from cooking either a ham or gammon,
1 really large Spanish onion, stuck with 4 cloves,
the outer parts of a large cleaned head of celery.

$\frac{1}{2}$ lb 12-hour soaked split peas,
2 unsalted pig's trotters,
one $1\frac{1}{2}$ lb knuckle of veal,
1 bouquet garni.

Taste chosen liquor. If only faintly salty, then reduce by simmering to taste. There should be at least 3 quarts at the finish. Add clove-stuck onion, trotters, knuckle and *bouquet garni*. Simmer until onion is really tender. Remove it, chop finely (discarding cloves), return to pan with strained, split peas and finely-chopped celery. Re-simmer until split peas collapse completely. Fish out trotters, knuckle and bouquet garni. Correct seasoning and serve with scraps of chopped trotter flesh.

117 Easter Soup

1½ pints well-reduced white
    bone stock,
4 oz minced or diced cooked
    chicken,
1 fat, trimmed, cleaned celery
    head,
¼ pint single cream,

salt and pepper,
optional crushed garlic clove,
1½ oz finely grated hard cheese,
celery salt.

Chop celery, poach in stock with crushed garlic until tender. Sieve, emulsify or liquidise. Re-heat to boiling, stir in cheese and chicken, continue stirring until cheese vanishes. Taste, correct seasoning, pour into heated bowls. When possible add a fat piped or spooned blob of whipped double or whipping cream to each serving. Sprinkle celery salt lightly overall.

118 Tschi (Russian Pot-au-Feu)

2 lb breast of mutton,
1 root of Florentine fennel,
10 peppercorns in scrap of
    butter muslin,
1 tiny cabbage,

6 medium carrots,
3 medium onions,
8 oz stoned, soaked prunes,
6 oz pearl barley,
salt.

Cut mutton into neat pieces. Pour on kettle of boiling water. Leave until cold, drain, wipe and put in an earthenware casserole with fennel, 1 teaspoonful salt and peppercorns. Cover well with cold water, bring to boil then skim. Add minced cabbage, carrots, and onions. Re-raise to boiling. Skim again, add pearl barley a second teaspoonful of salt and steady off at a simmer for 2 hours (or in oven, mid-shelf, for 3 hours at 335 F, (gas 3). Add prunes, simmer 45 mins, remove mutton, dice, discarding surplus fat, stir back into soup, checking that all bones and pepper bag have been removed. Taste, correct seasoning and serve.

*1 small halved, cleaned calf's
    head,
6 pints water,
2 large Spanish onions each
    stuck with 3 cloves,
leaf-tops and outside stems of
    1 celery head,
2 large lengthwise-quartered
    carrots.*

*1 large, trimmed, cleaned leek,
4 fat parsley stems,
salt and pepper,
2 oz dripping,
2 oz flour,
strained juice 1 lemon,
3 pints strong beef-bone stock.*

Simmer stock until reduced to mere ½ pint. Set aside. Simmer calf's
head in water with all vegetables cut into convenient pieces, and
parsley stems. Boil, skim thoroughly, set at steady simmer, maintain 2 hours. Strain through butter muslin over sieve, measure and
reduce by simmering to 4 pints. Make roux with dripping and flour.
Stir in reduced stock, gradually. Add chopped tongue and cheek
flesh and lemon juice. Taste, correct seasoning, optionally add 1
fluid oz dry Madeira, dry sherry or cooking-type brandy.

---

120 Potage des Abatis de Volaille (French Giblet Soup for
    Christmas)

*1¼ lb giblets and necks from
    Christmas bird,
1 diced medium onion,
1 crushed garlic clove,
1 coarsely grated large carrot,
1 torn bay leaf,
1 "leaf" lemon peel,
6 pints strong bone stock,*

*pepper and salt,
seasoned flour (page 18),
5½ oz finely diced pork fat,
3 crustless ½ inch thick bread
    slices,
4 dessertspoonsful concentrated
    tomato purée.*

Sizzle pork fat in frying pan over moderate heat. Turn giblets and
necks very liberally in seasoned flour. Fry in fat until well-browned,
over brisk heat. Lift out into a lidded casserole. Fry onion, carrot
and garlic in pan residue turning for 2 minutes. Scrape into casserole.
Add bay leaf, lemon peel, stock and cook under lid at 310 F (gas 2)
for 4/5 hours low down in oven, or until flesh collapses from bird
necks. Leave until cold. Remove top fat, strain soup. Pick meat

from necks, discard remainder except livers which are finely chopped. Remove bay leaf and lemon peel. Sieve, emulsify or liquidise meat with a little soup. Return to casserole, taste, correct seasoning, stir in tomato purée. Put skimmed fat into frying pan. When "singing", add diced given bread, fry until richly brown while stir/turning and hand separately.

121 Ham or Gammon Bone and Pea Soup

1 cooked ham or gammon bone, *1 small quartered carrot,*
2 quarts cleared pork bone stock, *1 crushed garlic clove,*
pea pods from 2 lb shelled peas, *1 medium, peeled, quartered*
6 bacon rinds,   *onion,*
pepper,   *1 sprig sage.*

Put all ingredients except pepper into roomy pan, bring to boil, steady off at simmer. Maintain 1½ hours. Strain, chop carrot and onion small, return to pan, add pepper to taste.

122 Scotch Broth

4 pints strong mutton bone stock, *1 outside stick celery,*
1 lb scrag end mutton,   *1 heaped dessertspoonful*
1 large onion,   *freshly milled parsley heads,*
1 trimmed leek,   *1 oz pearl barley,*
1 large carrot,   *salt and pepper,*
1 medium turnip,   *1 bouquet garni.*

Cut up meat, place in roomy pan with stock and 1 flat teaspoonful salt, simmer 2 hours. Rinse pearl barley thoroughly under cold water. Dice vegetables, add to stock with pearl barley and bouquet garni, simmer 1 hour. Strain, return liquor to pan, cut lean meat into dice from neck. At moment of service stir in with parsley, correct seasoning and serve.

123 Kidney Soup

3 pints beef stock,
½ lb ox kidney,
¼ lb shin of beef,
1½ oz dripping,
1 oz flour,

1 oz finely chopped onion,
1 flat tablespoonful freshly
    milled parsley,
salt and pepper.

Dice meat and kidney. Dissolve dripping in shallow pan, turn meats and onion in flour. Fry briskly, turning, for 3 minutes. Turn into roomy pan, cover with stock, simmer very gently 3 hours. Strain, add ¼ pint liquor to meat. Emulsify, liquidise or sieve, return to pan, simmer 20 minutes, stir in parsley, correct seasoning and serve.

Chinese and Japanese Soups

Chinese Stock
124. Three-Delicious Soup
Cream Stock
125. Special Chinese Cream of Spinach Soup
126. Simple Chinese Vegetable Soup
127. Chinese Egg Flower Soup
128. Chinese Bamboo-Shoot Soup
129. Chinese Crab and Sweet Corn Soup
130. Chinese Meat and Cucumber Soup
131. Peking Shrimp Soup
132. Chinese Fish Soup
133. Chinese Watercress Soup
134. Chinese Pork and Watercress Soup
135. Cantonese Vegetable Soup
136. Chinese Chicken Soup
137. Chinese Spare Ribs Soup
138. Chinese Fish Ball Soup
Chinese Fish Balls
139. Real Bird's Nest Soup
140. Chinese Cream of Shark's Fins Soup
141. Chinese Chicken Sesame Soup
142. Japanese Soy Soup
143. Yangtse Crab Soup
144. Chinese Liver and Tripe Soup
145. Asuka Nabe
146. Yasai-Suimono
147. Japanese Vegetable Soup

Chinese Stock

1 chicken carcase,
1 to 2 lb spare ribs,
4 pints cold water,

1 flat teaspoonful salt,
2 thin slices fresh root ginger.

Bring spare ribs, chicken carcase and water to boil. Remove scum as it rises, add salt and root ginger. Steady off at gentle simmer, maintain 1½ hours. Remove carcase and ribs, taste and, if needed, correct seasoning with more salt. This stock is used in a number of the following recipes.

Note: The special Chinese ingredients called for in some of these recipes (bird's nest, shark's fin, pickled mustard, salt cabbage, dried shrimps, bean curd, dried mushrooms, mirin, bonito shavings, shiritaki and fresh root ginger) are available from many large stores nowadays or from Oriental Store, 5, Macclesfield St, London, W.1.

124 Three-Delicious Soup (Chinese)

1 cooked chicken's breast from
   a 3 lb bird,
4 oz bean sprouts,
4 oz fresh unskinned button
   mushrooms,
1 teaspoonful sesame oil,

1 teaspoonful arrowroot,
2 pints stock,
1 tablespoonful sherry,
1 slightly rounded teaspoonful
   salt.

Discard skin from chicken's breast and underlying fillet piece. Slice flesh thinly into matchsticks. Slice the mushrooms and their stalks and mix with the bean sprouts and chicken. Take off a spoonful or two of stock to blend arrowroot to a thin paste and place the chicken and vegetables with the stock, ideally in a deepish pan with a well-fitting lid. When stock reaches boiling point uncovered, cover and simmer for 5 minutes. Uncover, add sherry and salt and then stir in the arrowroot dissolved to a runny paste with stock. Just stir for a moment or two until the soup thickens slightly, sprinkle with sesame oil, pour into soup bowls (ideally Chinese) and serve.

Note 1: This soup can be advance made and re-heated for service in a double saucepan over boiling water.

Note 2: The breasts of one small pigeon can replace the above given 1 chicken's breast.

Cream Stock

This is a luxurious, classic, ancient Chinese recipe for very special occasions only!

quarter of a 4/5 lb duck,
one 3½/4 lb roasting chicken,
½ lb pork rib bones,

4 thin slices fresh root ginger,
4 scallions or spring onions,
¾ lb tender, lean pork.

Cut through all joints of duck and chicken. Cut through wing, leg and drum-stick bones. Cut through rib bones of pork and slash meat with a sharp knife making several incisions to bones. Place all in a roomy pot or pan with 2 pints water, spring onions and ginger. Bring to boil, skim, steady off at simmer, maintain 20 minutes. Meanwhile, place 3 pints cold water in roomy bowl, remove stock from heat, strain, place a few pieces of meat and bones in cold water and rub through fingers breaking flesh back from bones. Drain and return to pot, bring to boil and simmer gently 1½ hours. Boil "rinse" water, skim and cool. Then remove meat and bones, cool them and take most of meat from bones. Skim stock, return bones and simmer steadily for 2½ hours with lid, to cause evaporation. Add a little of the "rinse" water gradually after 30 minutes. Cover a sieve with 2 folds butter-muslin and ladle stock through. Yield should be about 1 pint. Add 1 pint water to bones, bring to boil, strain through cheese-cloth, mix both lots together. When cold, remove fat layer from surface and use as instructed in recipe below. Withold seasoning until soup is completed.

---

125 Special Chinese Cream of Spinach Soup

½ lb picked, stalked, well
*   washed spinach,*

1¼ pints Cream Stock.

Shred spinach leaves to ¼ inch thickness. Heat cream stock, immerse spinach, bring to boil and serve.

---

126 Simple Chinese Vegetable Soup

4 oz shredded cabbage,
4 oz matchstick carrots,
1 oz chopped trimmed spring
  onions,
1 sprig thyme (leaves) chopped,
2 oz chopped onion,
1 fat head sage chopped,

1 skinned chopped tomato,
generous 1½ pints water,
2 fluid oz Soy sauce,
3 oz sliced mushroom stalks,
salt and pepper,
1 teaspoonful sesame oil.

Place all vegetables and herbs in roomy pan with water. Simmer until cabbage is just crisp, adding a little more water if desired when mixture becomes too thick. Stir in Soy, season to taste, stir in sesame oil and serve.

127 Chinese Egg Flower Soup (Soup of the Gods)

1 standard egg,
2 pints Chinese Stock
  (page 92),

1½ rounded tablespoonsful finely
  scissored chives,
1 coffeespoonful sesame oil.

Whip egg thoroughly. Bring stock to boil, steady off at simmer, trail beaten egg into soup over prongs of fork, in thin strands. Stir, add sesame oil, then chives.

128 Chinese Bamboo-Shoot Soup

¾ lb tinned bamboo-shoots,
1½ oz lean raw pork,
1½ oz raw unsalted pork fat,
2 tablespoonsful potato flour
  or arrowroot,
2 oz smoked ham or bacon,
2 pints Chinese Stock
  (page 92),

3 oz broccoli,
1 flat teaspoonful salt,
¼ teaspoonful Monosodium
  Glutamate (hereinafter
  called MSG),
2 tablespoonsful dry sherry,
1 teaspoonful sesame oil,
deep fryer and hot oil.

Slice bamboo-shoots into matchsticks. Do the same with ham or bacon and lean and fat of pork. Lengthwise split single sprigs of broccoli, in matchsticks. Turn lean and fat of pork in potato flour.

Heat Chinese Stock, add all prepared matchsticks except bamboo shoots, salt, raise to boiling point, steady off at simmer, maintain 10 minutes. Put prepared bamboo-shoots into frying basket, immerse in slightly smoking hot oil, fry 2 minutes. Turn on to absorbent kitchen paper. Add MSG and sherry to soup, simmer 2 minutes, stir in sesame oil and serve in lidded Chinese bowls, with bamboo shoots separately.

129 Chinese Crab and Sweet Corn Soup

4 pints Chinese Stock
  (page 92),
2 thin slices fresh root ginger,
one 8 oz tin sweet corn,
2 tablespoonsful dry sherry,
4 oz flaked white crab meat
  (tinned or fresh),
pepper,
1 flat tablespoonful potato flour
  or arrowroot,
4 tablespoonsful cold water,
1½ oz finely diced cooked ham,
1 rounded tablespoonful
  chopped chives.

Put ginger and stock into a pan, reduce by simmering to 2 pints. Stir in corn and finely flaked crab meat. When simmering steadily again, add pepper, sherry, blend chosen thickening agent with given cold water, stir, pour into soup, stir until this clears and serve with sprinklings of chives and ham on each portion.

130 Chinese Meat and Cucumber Soup

4 inches cut from unskinned
  cucumber,
1 oz lean pork,
1 oz pork fat,
1 rounded teaspoonful potato
  flour or arrowroot,
½ rounded teaspoonful salt,
generous pinch pepper,
4 pints Chinese Stock (page
  92), reduced by simmering
  to 1½ pints.

Cut cucumber with skin into matchsticks. Mix salt with potato flour, slice lean and pork fat into matchsticks, work thoroughly into potato flour. Raise stock to boiling point, add pork fat and lean, simmer 6 minutes, add cucumber, pepper to taste and simmer for 3 more minutes.

131 Peking Shrimp Soup

1 oz pure lard,
2 cakes bean curd,
4 Chinese dried mushrooms,
2 small shallots very finely
    chopped,
2 oz matchstick-cut bamboo-
    shoots or substituted bean
    sprouts,
2 pints chicken stock (A or B
    page 125),

2 oz fresh shelled shrimps,
2 tablespoonsful Soy sauce,
generous seasoning pepper,
3 tablespoonsful wine vinegar,
1 eggspoonful sesame oil,
1 oz cornflour,
3 tablespoonsful cold water,
1 standard egg.

Cube bean curd. Soak mushrooms in luke-warm water 15 minutes. Slice stems, quarter caps, reserve liquor. Dissolve lard in roomy pan, when "singing", add bamboo-shoots or bean sprouts, mushrooms and shallots. Stir/fry 2½ minutes. Add chicken stock, raise to boiling point, steady off at simmer, slide in bean curd, then shrimps. Re-raise to boiling point, stir in Soy sauce, wine vinegar, taste, season with pepper and simmer 4 minutes. Dissolve cornflour in given water, pour some soup on to cornflour, stir thoroughly, return to pan and stir carefully until mixture boils and thickens. Beat egg thoroughly, pour in thin stream over fork prongs so that strands form over soup surface. Add sesame oil and stir.

132 Chinese Fish Soup

6 dried mushrooms,
¼ lb haddock or pollock,
2 oz smoked ham or bacon,
3 white celery sticks,
2 oz carrots,
1 egg,
1 rounded tablespoonful
    cornflour,
4 tablespoonfuls water,
1 oz pure lard,
1 shallot very thinly sliced,

1 oz salt cabbage,
1 flat teaspoonful salt,
3 paper-thin slices root ginger,
2 pints chicken stock (A or B
    page 125),
1 tablespoonful Soy sauce,
2 tablespoonsful wine vinegar,
generous pinch white pepper,
1 teaspoonful sesame oil.

Soak mushrooms for 30 minutes, slice stems thinly and quarter caps. Cut ham or bacon into ¾ inch squares, celery into 1 inch lengths, and carrots paper thin. Whip egg thoroughly, heat lard in a thick roomy pan, when "singing" add shallot, carrot, ginger and celery and stir/fry about 3 minutes. Stir in ham or bacon, then salt cabbage, then mushrooms. Stir/fry for 2 minutes. Add stock and salt and raise to boiling point, steady off a simmer, maintain 4 minutes. Dice chosen fish into 1 inch boneless cubes, add to pan contents and when re-simmering, maintain 6 minutes. Trail in beaten egg across prongs of form, stir; stir in vinegar and corn-flour dissolved with given water. Taste, add pepper as desired, then stir in Soy sauce and sesame oil and serve at table from tureen.

---

133 Chinese Watercress Soup

1 standard bunch watercress,
2 oz cooked chicken's breast,
4 oz raw, lean ham or gammon,
1 level dessertspoonful potato
  flour or arrowroot,

1¾ pints chicken stock (see
  page 125),
1 flat teaspoonful salt,
1 teaspoonful melted chicken
  fat.

Cut ham into very slender strips. Place with stock in roomy pan. Bring to boil, simmer gently for 15 minutes. Cut main stalks from watercress, emulsify these with 4 tablespoonsful cold water, push with back of wooden spoon through strainer so that juice falls into soup. Pick off sprigs and green leaves, place in sieve, plunge into bowl of boiling water to blanch, then drain and divide between soup bowls. Remove cooked ham, weigh off 1 wiped ounce and keep for adding at service. Cut chicken into very thin strips, work potato flour or arrowroot into them. Return rest of ham to soup, stir in the 2 oz chicken, stir until thickened and clear, then add salt and allow to boil. Pour over watercress in the bowls and divide chicken fat into bowls. Float sprinklings of remaining ham on top.

134 Chinese Pork and Watercress Soup

3 oz lean raw pork,
½ flat teaspoonful salt,
2 slightly rounded tablespoonsful
   potato flour or arrowroot,

2 pints well-reduced Chinese
stock (page 92),
½ flat teaspoonful MSG,
1 bunch watercress,
pepper.

Rub pork with salt, cut into matchsticks, turn in potato flour or arrowroot. Raise stock to simmer, stir in MSG and pork and stir again. Simmer 10 minutes. Clean and pick watercress back to heads and leaves only, add to soup with pepper, simmer 4 minutes.

135 Cantonese Vegetable Soup

2½ pints Chinese stock, (page 92),
2 oz diced red of carrots,
2 oz diced turnips,
½ bunch watercress,
2 oz picked, stemmed, shredded
   spinach,
2 oz peeled marrow,

2 oz unskinned diced cucumber,
1 oz transparent Chinese
   noodles,
2 teaspoonsful Chinese shrimps,
1 flat teaspoonful salt,
pepper,
1 flat teaspoonful MSG.

Wash spinach, wash watercress and remove all stems. Heat stock, when boiling add turnips, carrots and shrimps. Simmer 15 minutes. Add diced marrow, watercress and noodles, after soaking noodles in boiling water 10 minutes, then add spinach and cucumber; simmer 5 minutes. Sprinkle with salt and MSG, taste, add pepper as desired.

136 Chinese Chicken Soup

4 oz raw white chicken breast,
   sliced paper-thin and then
   into fine strips,
3 oz bamboo-shoots or bean
   sprouts,
1 egg,
2 thin slices root ginger,
1 flat teaspoonful salt,

1¾ pints chicken stock (A or B
   page 125),
oil in deep fryer,
2 rounded teaspoonsful chicken
   fat,
2 rounded teaspoonsful potato
   flour,
2 tablespoonsful cold water,
½ flat teaspoonful MSG.

Whip egg, add half to chicken strips, blend thoroughly, add half potato flour, turn over and put into heated, oily fry basket. When oil reaches 385 F immerse basket, count 10 fairly fast, raise basket, turn contents on to absorbent kitchen paper. Heat chicken stock to boiling, simmer, remove scum, add salt, ginger, MSG and shredded bamboo-shoots or bean sprouts. Simmer 4 minutes. Dissolve remaining potato flour in cold water, stir into soup, scatter in fried chicken, stir in chicken fat and serve.

137 Chinese Spare Ribs Soup

½ lb lean, divided spare ribs,
2½ pints Chinese stock
   (page 92),
1 large stem pickled mustard
   or substitute 2 fat spring
   onions,

1 eggspoonful castor sugar,
2 little cakes bean curd,
salt and pepper,
1 mean flat teaspoonful MSG.

Place stock, sugar and mustard or spring onions in pan. Cover spare ribs in roomy bowl with cold water, leave 10 minutes. Drain and add to soup. Maintain at simmer for 1½ hours, taste, correct seasoning and finally stir in neatly cubed bean curd.

138 Chinese Fish Ball Soup

1 pint chicken stock (A or B
   page 125),
1½ oz finely sliced bamboo-
   shoots or bean sprouts,
6 medium dried mushrooms,
1 flat eggspoonful MSG,

2 scallions or spring onions,
½ oz raw, minutely diced,
   unsalted pork fat,
salt and pepper,
Chinese Fish Balls (page 100).

Bring stock to boiling point, add salt, MSG, bamboo-shoots or bean sprouts and quartered, stalks sliced, previously soaked mushrooms. Trim, wash and chop spring onions into 1 inch lengths, add with pork fat, taste, correct seasoning and maintain at steady simmer for 8 minutes. Pour over a few fish balls in each soup bowl and serve.

Chinese Fish Balls

1 lb haddock or smoked cod
 fillet,
1 oz finely chopped shallot or
 small onion,
1 oz finely chopped lean bacon,

2 thin slices finely chopped
 fresh root ginger,
salt and pepper,
1 tablespoonful dry sherry.

Soak chosen salt fish in cold water for 1 hour. Drain, wipe and rough cut. Place in emulsifier or liquidiser with 2 fluid oz water and whip at full until creamy. Add 2 generous pinches salt and 1 of pepper, continue emulsifying for a further 7 minutes adding a few drips more water if required. When thoroughly creamy, work in onion, ham, ginger and sherry. Shape into small walnuts, roll between palms, refrigerate 30 minutes to harden, then drop into roomy pan of slightly-simmering salted water. Leave until all are risen and cooked, for 7/8 minutes. Drain, divide between soup bowls, cover with soup and serve.

139 Real Bird's Nest Soup

5 oz bird's nest,
4 oz minced white of chicken,
2 oz lean, minced ham,
2 separated egg whites,
1 fluid oz and 1 pint chicken
 stock

1 fluid oz dry sherry,
salt and pepper,
2 finely chopped scallions or
 spring onions.

Soak bird's nest overnight in abundant cold water. Drain, wipe and simmer gently from cold water to boil and then for 20 minutes in water to cover. Leave undisturbed until cold. Blend minced chicken with sherry and stock. Whip egg whites for 1½ minutes at full mixer speed. Beat in chicken, drain bird's nest, place with chicken stock in pan, season to taste, add spring onions, raise to boiling point and simmer gently for 12 minutes. Draw and stir egg white/chicken mix slowly into soup with fork. Stir while returning to boiling point, sprinkle with ham and serve.

140 Chinese Cream of Shark's Fins Soup

¼ lb dried shark's fins,
1½ pints Cream Stock
  (page 93),

cold water,
2 peeled finely sliced Spanish
  onions.

Place shark's fins in 3 pints cold water. Change water every 8 hours for 24 hours. Heat 2 quarts water with onions, simmer 10 minutes. Drain fins, rinse well in more cold water. Cover with Cream Stock, add onions then simmer for 2 hours extremely gently with asbestos mat between flame and pan base. Fins should be tender and slightly crunchy.

141 Chinese Chicken Sesame Soup

1 cooked chicken breast,
4 oz bean sprouts,
4 oz mushrooms,
1 teaspoonful sesame oil,

1 teaspoonful arrowroot,
2 pints stock,
1 tablespoonful sherry,
1 teaspoonful salt.

Slice breast thinly into matchsticks. Slice un-skinned mushrooms and stalks thinly. Mix with bean sprouts and chicken. Blend arrowroot with a little of given stock. Put chicken mix into stock in roomy, lidded pan. When boiling, cover and simmer for 5 minutes. Add sherry and salt and arrowroot paste. Stir until soup thickens a little, then sprinkle with sesame oil, stir again and serve.

142 Japanese Soy Soup

¼ teacup mirin,
4 fluid oz Soy sauce,

8 fluid oz water,
½ oz dried bonito shavings.

Bring mirin to boiling point in given water, add Soy and bonito, boil again, remove from heat, strain and serve.

143 Yangtse Crab Soup

This, when made authentically, uses the tiny crabs for which the Yangtse River is famous. Our kind of crab meat makes a good substitute.

½ lb crab meat, flaked,
1 oz finely diced pork fat,
1 oz finely chopped cooked ham,
2 finely chopped shallots,
salt and pepper,
1 scant flat teaspoonful MSG,

1 pint chicken stock (A or B page 125),
1 fluid oz dry sherry,
¼ pint milk (top-of-the-milk is even better),
1 rounded dessertspoonful potato flour or arrowroot.

Place chosen stock in roomy pan, add shallots and simmer down to ¾ pint. Stir in sherry, salt and pepper to taste, MSG, and chosen thickening blended with milk. Stir until smoothly thickened, add crab meat, simmer on 4 minutes, turn into soup-bowls, sprinkle tops with ham and pork fat.

144 Chinese Liver and Tripe Soup

4 slim leeks, shredded,
4 oz tripe soaked in salted water 1 hour,
1 flat teaspoonful salt,
1 oz finely-chopped shallot or onion,
3 oz finely-scissored chickens' livers,
1 oz dry cooking sherry,
1 tablespoonful wine vinegar,

1 thin slice root ginger,
1 tablespoonful Soy sauce,
2¼ pints Chinese stock, well-reduced, (page 92),
½ flat teaspoonful MSG,
1 oz melted chicken or pork fat,
3–4 oz double or honeycomb tripe,
pepper.

Note: In absence of tripe, increase chickens' livers proportionally.

Slice tripe into fat matchsticks, soak, drain, wipe and use. Plunge prepared liver and tripe into boiling water. Leave 40 minutes. Drain, wipe. Place in roomy bowl with sherry, pepper, Soy sauce, vinegar, stir well. Heat chosen fat in roomy pan, add shallot or onion and leeks, stir/fry until thoroughly yellowed. Add liquor, MSG, simmer 10 minutes. Add liver and tripe, simmer 4 minutes, add chopped ginger, taste, correct seasoning and serve.

145 Asuka Nabe (Japanese Soup)

1 small spring chicken,
2 pints water,
8 scalded, stemmed, unskinned
  mushrooms,
1 carrot, pared into shavings,
½ lb shiritaki

1 small head steamed Chinese
  cabbage,
¼ lb picked de-stemmed spinach,
1¼ pints milk,
2 flat teaspoonsful salt,
1 tablespoonful Soy sauce,
½ flat teaspoonful castor sugar.

Pare all raw chicken flesh from bones, cut in 1 inch pieces. Chop bones into 1 inch pieces. Sink into almost boiling water, boil, skim and strain. Par-boil carrot shavings in chicken water 10 minutes, strain, repeat with shiritaki, strain. Steam Chinese cabbage 6 minutes. Steam spinach leaves 4 minutes, sink both in cold water, wipe, wrap spinach around cabbage and cut into 1 inch rounds. Pour stock into clean pan. Add chicken flesh and sliced cabbage. Cook 4 minutes, skim, add milk, Soy, sugar, then thinly-sliced mushrooms and carrot, cook 6 minutes over medium heat. Divide cooked solids between individual bowls. Cover with soup liquor, add extra light sprinkling of pepper.

146 Yasai-Suimono (Japanese Vegetable Soup)

2 oz Chinese dried mushrooms,
3 pints chicken stock (A or B
  page 125),
½ lb tender, lean pork cut
  hair-thin,
1 carrot cut hair-thin,

1 small tin bean sprouts,
1 tablespoonful Soy sauce,
3–4 oz finely shredded raw
  spinach leaves,
1 rounded teaspoonful powdered
  ginger.

Place dried mushrooms in enough chicken stock to cover. Steep 1 hour. Drain, slice thinly, place in roomy pan with remainder of chicken stock and steeping liquid, add pork, boil then simmer over low heat 10 minutes. Add carrot, bean sprouts and Soy. Simmer 5 minutes. Shred stemless spinach finely. Add to soup with ginger, raise to fast rolling boil, cook 2 minutes, stir and serve in bowls. This soup may also have Drunken Prawns (page 15) as side accompaniment.

147 Japanese Vegetable Soup

2 oz mushrooms, sliced,
48 fluid oz stock,
$\frac{1}{2}$ lb lean pork, diced,
1 carrot cut into matchsticks,

one $9\frac{1}{2}$ oz tin bean sprouts,
1 tablespoonful Soy sauce,
3–4 oz raw spinach,
1 teaspoonful powdered ginger.

Place mushrooms and pork in stock. Bring to the boil and simmer for 10 minutes. Add carrots, bean sprouts, spinach and Soy sauce. Cook for further 5 minutes. Finally add ginger.

Fish Soups

Basic Fish Stock

2 pints cold water,
1½ lb fish trimmings (e.g. sole,
   plaice or whiting carcase,
   skin, head),
1 large "leaf" of thinly-cut
   lemon peel,
2 crushed peppercorns,

1 herb faggot comprising 1 bay
   leaf, 4 parsley stalks, 1 small
   sprig thyme, 1 crushed fennel
   seed or 1 small sprig fresh
   fennel when available.

Place all ingredients in roomy pan. Bring to the boil briskly, skim thoroughly, steady off at simmer and maintain for 20 minutes. Strain and use as instructed in individual recipes.

148 Aigo-Sau (Provençale White Fish Soup)

1 lb any skinned, boned white
   fish,
1 large minced onion,
peeled flesh of 2 large de-seeded
   and cored tomatoes,
5 small peeled, quartered
   potatoes,
2 peeled garlic cloves,

1 herb faggot comprising
   fennel, bay, thyme, celery,
   parsley stalks,
salt and pepper,
1 tablespoonful olive oil,
Pulled Bread (page 12),
optional Rouille (see below),
salt and pepper.

Place fish in roomy pan, add all other ingredients, bring to boil, skim, simmer gently 30 minutes. Correct seasoning. Ladle into heated bowls. Hand Pulled Bread separately and optionally *La Rouille*.

La Rouille

This very special Provençale sauce is either stirred in minute quantities into soup before drinking or spread thinly on pieces of Pulled Bread and then floated on soup.

2 peeled garlic cloves,
2 large pimentoes (fresh or
   tinned),
1 separated egg yolk,

3 tablespoonsful olive oil and as
   much soft, fine white breadcrumbs as will make a stiff
   paste,
2 tablespoonsful completed fish
   soup.

De-seed and de-pith fresh pimentoes, then skin halves by grilling until skins brown and peel off. Pound garlic cloves, pimentoes and 1 tablespoonful of oil with breadcrumbs using mortar and working hard—it must be a smooth paste. Once a paste has been achieved, work in egg yolk, pound in remaining oil drop by drop until mixture assumes texture of mayonnaise. You can do this an alternative way by omitting breadcrumbs altogether and just pounding pimentoes and garlic to paste, then working in olive oil and soup. The first method is easier, the second better—you choose.

149 Crème de Moules au Riz

Follow recipe for Soupe aux Moules et Riz (page 109) to completion, strain, stir in $\frac{1}{4}$ pint boiling single cream. Add 1 heape d dessertspoonful milled fresh parsley heads and serve with hot French bread.

150 Soupe au Crabe

$\frac{3}{4}$ lb white and brown crab meat,
1 tablespoonful wine vinegar,
1 tablespoonful strained lemon
   juice,
3 peppercorns,
1 small, torn bay leaf,
5 fluid oz dry white cooking-
   type wine,
$\frac{1}{4}$ pint single cream,
water,

1 rounded dessertspoonful
   freshly milled parsley heads,
1 lb white fish trimmings,
1 oz butter,
1 generous tablespoonful
   cooking-type brandy,
4 parsley stalks,
pepper,
1 large "leaf" lemon peel.

Place fish trimmings in roomy pan with lemon peel, parsley stalks, bay leaf, peppercorns, wine vinegar, and cold water to cover completely. Raise to boil, steady off at simmer, skim off any risen scum, maintain for a clear 20 minutes. Strain, return liquor to clean pan, simmer down to $1\frac{3}{4}$ pints. Add wine. Mix white and brown crab meats. Weigh off 2 oz and roll into pea-sized balls. Stir remainder into reduced, strained stock with wine. Stir/simmer 3 minutes, add brandy then cream, taste, add pepper, serve in bowls with a few crab meat balls floating on top of each. Optionally sprinkle with milled parsley.

151 Finnish Salmon Soup

5 pints simple fish stock
  (see below),
4 slices tail-of-salmon,
4 sprigs dill,

4 wooden cocktail sticks,
salt and pepper,
2½ oz butter.

Assemble salmon slices by laying sprig of dill* between each and securing all four slices together with cocktail sticks. Set in roomy pan with stock, add light seasonings of salt and pepper and simmer gently until salmon is thoroughly cooked. Remove. Simmer hard now to reduce to half quantity, i.e. 2½ pints. Stir in butter in small flakes. Divide salmon slices into neat pieces. Return to soup, simmer until salmon is just heated through again and serve.

*When dill unavailable, replace with fennel.

Simple Fish Stock

2 lb fish trimmings (tails, spine
  bones, skins and fins),
6 pints water,
thin peel 1 medium lemon,
1 torn bay leaf,
1 sprig thyme,
4 peppercorns,

6 parsley stalks,
2 outside sticks celery rough-
  chopped,
strained juice 1 medium lemon,
¼ pint inexpensive, dry white
  cooking wine or cider.

Place all ingredients except wine or cider in roomy pan, bring to boil, skim and simmer 20 minutes. Strain, add wine or cider and use.

152 Soupe aux Moules et Riz

3 pints scrubbed, bearded
   mussels,
2 fat parsley stalks,
1 torn bay leaf,
3 skinned de-pipped tomatoes,
1 fluid oz olive oil,
salt and pepper,

1 pinch saffron,
the white and green of 2 slim
   leeks, thinly sliced,
3 oz rice,
2 pints fish stock (page 106),
¼ pint dry white cooking wine,
2 shallots.

Steam mussels until opened, remove empty half-shells. Dice fine
and then fry shallots and leeks in hot oil. When nearly soft, add
tomatoes, turn into roomy pan. Add parsley and bay, salt, pepper,
cover with stock, simmer 10 minutes, stir in rice and saffron, simmer
steadily 11½ mins, add wine and mussels, raise to boiling, simmer
2 more minutes. Remove parsley stalks, bay, and serve.

153 Modest Fish Soup

1 lb white fish trimmings, (skins,
   bones, fins, tails, heads),
¼ lb smoked haddock fillet,
1 oz butter,
1 separated egg yolk,
1 fine-grated shallot or small
   onion,
1 torn bay leaf,

3 peppercorns,
1 "leaf" lemon peel,
2 parsley stalks,
water,
¼ pint top-of-milk or single
   cream,
1 rounded dessertspoonful
   freshly milled parsley.

Place fish trimmings, shallot, bay, peppercorns, lemon peel and
parsley stalks in pan and cover generously with cold water. Simmer
20 minutes fairly strongly. Strain, add diced boned haddock to
liquor, simmer 20 minutes more. Remove fish, flake finely, removing
skin, return to liquor. Stir egg yolk with cream, ladle on a little
soup, stir again, turn into pan and stir carefully without allowing
mix to boil. Taste, add butter and more pepper if desired. Stir in
parsley and serve.

154 Clam Chowder

15 fluid oz fish stock (page 106),
5 fluid oz cooking-type dry
  white wine,
1 flat dessertspoonful freshly
  milled parsley heads,
1 shallot,
4 smallish potatoes,

1 crushed garlic clove,
½ pint milk or single cream,
2 oz butter,
1 pint clams (or equivalent
  from tin),
pepper.

Chop shallot finely with potatoes, crush garlic. Simmer clams in shell in stock under lid until open. Cool, remove clams from shells or *start here with tinned ones.* Chop clams, add with their liquor to other prepared items, put in strained stock, add wine, then butter, then milk or cream, and parsley. Simmer 40 minutes gently. Taste, correct seasoning and serve.

155 Waterzootje

(Introduced into England during the reign of King William III.)

4 small ½ inch thick "steaks"
  cut from salmon tail,
1 large scraped, sliced carrot,
4 trimmed scraped/sliced
  parsley roots,
pepper and salt,

½ pint dry, white, cooking-type
  wine,
2 pints fish stock (page 106),
1 rounded tablespoonful fresh
  milled parsley,
4 parsley stalks,
1 leaf of lemon rind.

Trim "steaks" and put trimmings and tail into a roomy pan with prepared carrot, parsley root, stock and lemon rind. Bring to the boil then simmer very gently for 30 minutes. Lift salmon in separate pan. Pour stock mixture through strainer on to salmon. Add parsley stalks and wine. Simmer extremely gently for 9 minutes. Stir in milled parsley, taste, correct seasoning and, according to tradition, eat with a dessertspoon and fork with very thin slices of new brown bread, crusts left on and liberally buttered.

156 Pollock and Shrimp Soup

½ oz butter,
½ oz flour,
¼ pint brown shrimps in shells,
6 oz pollock,
1¼ pints milk,
2 parsley stalks,
1 "leaf" of lemon peel,

1 heaped teaspoonful milled
   parsley heads,
1 heaped teaspoonful finely
   scissored chives,
1 sprig fennel (when available),
1 generous teaspoonful anchovy
   purée.

Shell shrimps, reserving shells. Place milk, shrimp-shells, parsley stalks, lemon peel and fennel in a pan. Steam cubed raw pollock. Bring milk mixture to boil, simmer for 20 minutes. Strain, discard fennel, lemon peel and shrimp shells. Stir in anchovy purée. Dissolve butter in small pan. Stir in flour. When soft ball is formed add all milk mixture gradually, beating very smooth between each addition. Return fish to pan, add shelled shrimps, parsley and chives and hand oven-crisp ¼ inch thick slices French bread separately for immersing in each serving.

157 Iced Seafood Soup

2¼ pints water,
1 large "leaf" lemon peel,
3 parsley stems,
1 torn bay leaf,
¼ pint brown shrimps,
¼ pint pink shrimps,
6 fluid oz modest, dry white wine,

¼ pint single cream,
½ pint best milk,
2 oz brown crab meat,
2 oz white crab meat,
1 lb white fish trimmings,
pepper.

Shell shrimps, reserving shells. Put trimmings, shrimp shells, peel, parsley, bay leaf and water into pan, bring to boil, simmer fairly fast 20 minutes. Strain and return to pan. Add wine, allow to boil, add milk, repeat, stir in cream, all but a few shrimps and all crab-meat. Taste, correct pepper seasoning, chill until required. Drop 1/2 ice cubes into each bowl, pour in icy soup, optionally scatter tops with chives, parsley or light sprinkling of scissored dill and remaining shrimps.

158 American Fish Chowder

2 lb cod, haddock or pollock,	salt and pepper,
1½ oz fine-diced pork fat,	6 crumbled cream crackers,
1½ pints fish stock (page 106),	1¼ lb diced old potatoes,
1 pint milk,	1½ oz butter,
6 fluid oz single cream,	1 medium chopped onion.

Steam fish, cool, skin and bone. Break up fish into small pieces. Sizzle pork fat dice in roomy pan, add onion and stir/turn until golden. Add fish stock, milk, potatoes and fish, simmer 12 minutes, stir in cream, correct seasoning, stir in butter until dissolved, and serve piping hot in bowls with cracker crumbs sprinkled over each portion.

159 Greek Fish Soup

1 lb pollock, haddock or bass,	3 flat tablespoonsful
1 small cod's head,	concentrated tomato purée,
1 medium onion,	1½ oz flour,
1 medium leek,	¼ pint milk,
1 outside stick celery,	2 heaped tablespoonsful flour,
3 parsley stalks,	1 sprig fennel,
1 small, crushed garlic clove,	grated rind 1 lemon,
5 fluid oz modest white wine,	salt,
	3 peppercorns.

Place fish in cold water to cover with cod's head, chopped onion, leek, celery, parsley stalks, peppercorns. Simmer gently until all fish is tender. Remove cod's head, remove cheek flesh and set this aside. Simmer on fairly hard with all removed skins and bones taken from fish, for 20 minutes. Strain, measure and add lemon peel, tomato purée, fennel, further reduce by simmering to 2½ pints. Remove fennel, stir wine gradually on to flour and when made into thin paste stir back into soup. Simmer until all taste of flour is eliminated, taste, correct seasoning, flake fish flesh finely, return to soup and when boiling serve with stirred-in parsley and Pulled Bread (page 12).

160 Poor Man's Chowder

8 oz fresh haddock,
5 medium potatoes,
1 large onion,
2 pints fish stock,

salt and pepper,
½ pint top-of-the-milk or single
   cream,
1 rounded tablespoonful freshly
   milled parsley heads.

Divide haddock into neat, boneless cubes. Peel potatoes, and dice with onion. Add both to stock, bring to boil, skim, simmer very gently 45 minutes. Add haddock, simmer on 20 minutes. Stir in cream, correct seasoning, add parsley and serve with Pulled Bread (page 12).

161 Cod's Head Soup

2 oz butter or 1 oz dripping and
   1 oz oil,
5 oz finely chopped onion,
2 oz flour,
1 flat teaspoonful Masala paste,
1 sprig thyme,
salt and pepper,
1 medium cod's head,

5 pints fish stock,(page 106),
1 bay leaf,
thin peel from ½ lemon,
1 small sprig fennel or dill,
6 oz over-ripe, rough-cut
   unskinned tomatoes,
4 parsley stalks,
1 rounded dessertspoonful finely
   milled parsley.

Heat chosen fat. When "singing" stir in onion and cook very gently for 10 minutes. Work in Masala paste and flour. Work in 1 pint fish stock until smooth. Turn into large pot or pan. Add all remaining ingredients except seasoning and parsley heads. Bring to boil, skim, simmer very gently 3 hours. Strain through muslin, pick out best flesh from cod's head cheeks, flake, add to strained soup, taste, correct seasoning, add parsley and serve with croûtons (page 17).

162 Quick Cream of Crab Soup

one 8 oz tin crab meat, picked
and flaked,
2 small hard-boiled eggs chopped
finely,
salt and pepper,
pinch of allspice,

1 rounded tablespoonful butter,
1 large lemon sliced thinly,
and de-pipped,
1 quart boiling milk,
6 large cracker biscuits
crumbled coarsely.

Put crab meat and liquor into milk, and begin simmering over a moderate heat. Add seasonings to taste and spice, then add butter in small flakes. After 15 minutes add cracker crumbs and chopped eggs. Line out a tureen with lemon slices. Pour on soup and hand more buttered cracker biscuits separately, which have been optionally spread lightly with anchovy purée.

163 Potage à la Grecque

4 very thinly-sliced large
shallots or small onions,
1½ oz butter,
¼ flat coffeespoonful pepper,
1 oz flour,
2 pounded peppercorns,
3 raw, sliced tomatoes,
1 herb faggot,
6 small, washed, wiped anchovy
fillets,

4 oz steamed fresh haddock
(free of skin and bone),
1½ pints fish stock (page 106)
and ¼ pint white wine or use
1¾ pints stock,
1 or 2 drops liquid carmine for
colouring,
½ pint top-of-milk or single
cream.

Flake haddock finely. Dissolve butter in frying pan and fry onions under lid very gently for 20 minutes, checking they do not brown. When tender shake flour and pepper over them. Stir/press with wooden spoon until a light paste forms. Work in the wine or first ¼ pint stock. Add finely chopped anchovies and tomato slices,

114

scrape into a saucepan, stir in all remaining fluid except cream, add faggot, simmer 35 minutes and remove faggot. Add haddock, then emulsify. Return to pan. Colour with carmine and stir in boiling cream. Hand small crustless triangular bread pieces which have been fried briskly in an extra 1 oz oil, and spread lightly with optional Garlic Butter (page 18).

---

164 Soupe Andalouse

½ pint Soubise (onion) Sauce
  (page 17),
½ pint tomato pulp,
4 oz raw whiting or fresh
  haddock flesh,
1 oz rice flour,
½ flat saltspoonful pepper,
strained juice of ½ lemon,

5 fluid oz dry white cooking
  wine,
1½ pints fish stock (page 106)
  or 1¾ pints stock,
2 separated egg yolks,
¼ pint single cream,
salt to season.

Poach fish in stock until tender. Remove any skin and bone, flake finely and put into roomy pan with Soubise, tomato pulp, pepper, lemon juice, strained stock and wine. Dust rice flour over surface, stir and simmer gently for 40 minutes, giving an occasional stir. Emulsify, return to pan, stand over hot water in outer container (au bain marie) using as substitute an ordinary meat baking tin half-filled with boiling water set over moderate heat. Blend cream and egg yolks carefully. Ladle on a little soup. Stir well, scrape into pan and stir again then allow to cook for a few moments until liaison is complete and soup has thickened slightly. Taste, correct seasoning and serve.

Note: In the original of this very fine soup cooked, freshwater crayfish bodies were simmered in fish stock, shelled and sliced into small rounds and floated upon each serving in its bowl.

165 Crème aux Fruits de Mer (Modest)

6 oz mixed brown and white crab
  meat,
1 lb white fish trimmings,
¼ pint modest dry white wine,
4 oz shelled shrimps (keep
  shells),
2 pints cold water,
1 small sprig fennel (when
  possible),

2 parsley stalks,
1 small, torn bay leaf,
1 large "leaf" of lemon peel,
2 peppercorns,
2 tablespoonsful cooking
  brandy,
4 fluid oz whipping cream,
extra top-of-milk.

Put fish trimmings and shrimp shells with bay leaf, fennel, parsley stalks, lemon peel and peppercorns into roomy pan. Add water and bring to boil. Skim, then simmer on for 20 minutes. Strain very thoroughly. Stir in wine and brandy, crabmeats and 3 oz of shrimps; then add top-of-milk to achieve desired consistency—creamily loose and comfortable to drink. Whip up the whipping cream to a strong peak. At the moment of service pour soup into heated bowls. Scatter one or two shrimps over each serving. Blob cream on top and optionally scatter finely-scissored chives overall.

166 Eel Soup

1 lb skinned, jointed eel,
2 medium shallots or 1 onion,
  peeled and finely sliced,
3 pints fish stock (page 106),
¼ pint single cream,

salt and pepper,
1 heaped tablespoonful milled
  fresh parsley heads,
½ oz butter,
½ oz oil.

Dissolve butter and heat oil in shallow pan. Toss in eel pieces, fry briskly until well-browned all over. Turn into roomy pan, add stock, bring to boil, skim and simmer gently for 1 hour. Strain stock back into clean pan, taste, correct seasoning. Cut eel flesh from bones, chop finely, add to stock, simmer 20 minutes, stir in cream and stir in parsley at moment of service.

167 New Orleans Gumbo

1 lb mixed white and brown
   crab meat,
1 medium finely chopped onion
   or 2 small shallots,
6 large, ripe, peeled de-seeded
   tomatoes,
1 quart tin of drained, washed
   sliced okra,

1 torn bay leaf,
1 largeish sprig thyme or
   lemon thyme,
3½ pints fish stock (page 106),
1 tablespoonful Filé,
½ lb long-grained rice,
2 oz oil.

Heat oil until it "sings", fry onions under lid over low heat until tender but not browned. Add crab meat, stir in very thoroughly, add tomatoes and sliced lengthwise okra and simmer on for 10 minutes stirring frequently. Scrape into a roomy pan, add all fish stock and herbs, stir and simmer gently for 35 minutes. Fish out herbs, add Filé, stir well and serve with a tablespoon of rice in the bottom of each bowl and the remainder handed separately. Have ready plenty of slightly-salted, fast-bubbling water. Add rice, stir until water re-bubbles, then maintain for 11½ minutes and strain.

168 Waterzootje of Char

Follow instructions for Waterzootje (page 110) replacing salmon with four ¼ inch slices cut from tail of a small char. This variable member of Balu family is held in high estreem by fishermen and is found in the Lake District.

169 Soupe au Moules Chivry

Copy recipe for Velouté Chivry (page 64) as far as blending in of Velouté, then toss in 2 dozen well-scrubbed and bearded mussels, simmer fast for 3 minutes. Discard closed shells, remove mussels from opened shells and finish as for Velouté Chivry.

170 Simple Fish Soup

1 lb cod, hake or pollock,
1 quart water or fish stock,
salt and pepper,
4 medium potatoes coarse-
grated,
1 rasher diced streaky bacon,

1 very thinly sliced medium
onion,
4 parsley stalks,
1 tablespoonful finely scissored
chives,
1 thread saffron or a half
thimbleful.

Poach fish in stock or water, until tender. Remove, cool, skin, and then divide into cubes. Add vegetables, bacon, stalks and saffron to fish liquor. Simmer for 30 minutes remove stalks, add chives and serve with oven baked $\frac{1}{4}$ inch slices cut from a long thin loaf ("flute"). Bread should be baked hard. Have bowl of grated hard cheese. Each person floats 3 or 4 croûtons on soup in soup plates and sprinkles these with cheese.

171 Soupe de Poisson (a luxury)

Unlike Bouillabaisse, this fish soup can be made in England, not requiring the 14 different Mediterranean fish essential to Bouillabaisse!

1 quart mussels,
$\frac{1}{2}$ pint shelled grey or pink
shrimps,
1 doz small, fresh prawns,
1 envelope or thimble of saffron,
4 parsley stalks,
4 medium tomatoes, skinned
and chopped,
2 lb white fish trimmings,
2 sole or plaice fillets,

1 large red pimento, finely
sliced,
2 garlic cloves,
2 rounded tablespoonsful
freshly milled parsley,
4 tablespoonsful olive oil,
$\frac{1}{2}$ pint dry white wine,
5 pints cold water,
4 peppercorns,
1 large "leaf" lemon peel.

Put shrimp shells and fish trimmings into pan with saffron, parsley stalks, lemon peel, peppercorns (remembering to crush one only). Cover with cold water, bring to boil, maintain 20 minutes at bubbling simmer. Escoffier ruled that after that, you actually boil out the flavour of fish stock! Leave until cold, strain thoroughly, pressing down in sieve with back of wooden spoon. Scrub, beard and steam mussels under lid 3 minutes. Discard any which remain closed. Remove all empty half-shells from opened ones. Cut chosen fillets into slender strips. Turn strained liquor into roomy pan, add white wine, pimento, crushed garlic, tomatoes, oil, shelled shrimps, unshelled prawns (classic) or shelled prawns (optional). Bring to boil, slide in mussels and fish strips. Simmer 4 minutes. Turn into heated tureen. Heat roomy soup bowls, fill, scatter parsley overall, serve at table with plenty of hot French bread or Garlic Bread (page 13).

Clear Soups

Consommé
172. Real Consommé
173. 2nd Level Consommé
174. Consommé en Gelée (from a tin)
Basic Bone Stock
Oven Made Stock
Chicken Stock A and B
175. Clear Hare Soup
176. Brown Soup Stock (Bouillon)
177. Consommé en Gelée
178. Fake Consommé
179. Fake Consommé en Gelée
180. The Service of Tinned Turtle Soup
181. Petite Marmite
182. Poule au Pot
183. Bouillon de Boeuf
184. Bouillon Czarina
185. Bouillon Ferneuse
186. Zuppa Pavese
187. Consommé aux Tomates
188. Consommé de Laitues
189. Consommé Colnet
190. Consommé à la Colbert
191. Consommé au Cresson Alenois
192. Consommé de Volaille aux Diablotins
193. Consommé à la Bourgeoise
194. Consommé Brillat-Savarin
195. Consommé Chasseur
196. Consommé à la Chilienne
197. Consommé aux Piments Doux
198. Consommé à la Portugaise
199. Consommé de Volaille Napolitaine
200. Consommé Brancas
201. Minestra Mille Fanti
202. Consommé aux Trois Filets
203. Consommé aux Profiteroles
204. Consommé au Parmesan
205. Consommé à la Royale de Tomate
206. Consommé à la Royale d'Epinards
207. Consommé Xavier

[continued]

208. Consommé à la Madrilene
209. Consommé à l'Aurore
210. Consommé Glacé à l'Estragon
211. Consommé à la Parisienne
212. Consommé à la Royale
213. Consommé de Poisson
214. Consommé Kandourow
215. Consommé de Poisson Normande
216. Consommé de Poisson aux Crevettes
217. Consommé Hollandaise
218. Consommé d'Homard
219. Consommé aux Moules
220. Consommé à l'Orge du Perles
221. Consommé à la Florentine
222. Consommé Florette
223. Consommé aux Gombos à l'Orientale
224. Consommé au Macaroni
225. Consommé Mercedes
226. Consommé de Racines Fraiches
227. Consommé Julienne
228. Pot-au-Feu à la Languedocienne
229. Consommé Hudson
230. Curry and Apple Soup
231. Consommé de Concombre
232. Consommé au Fumet des Fines Herbes
233. Cornish Kiddley Broth
234. Game Consommé
235. Chicken Consommé
236. Consommé Vert Pré
237. Consommé à l'Essence de Celeri

Consommé

First let us understand the meaning of the word. On the highest level this is crystal clear, pale gold fluid which, if allowed to chill sets into light jelly. If served hot, the ultimate test of quality is for it to be tacky on the lips. There are game, poultry and veal consommés both hot and "en gelée" which is self explanatory. The suffixes attached to the names on classic menus, indicate the nature of the garnish or flavouring.

Example (flavouring) Consommé Xeres (Xeres = sherry).

Example (garnish) Consommé Royale (with egg).

172 Real Consommé

5½ pints beef, veal or
  chicken stock,
1 lb rump steak, finely chopped,
2 separated unbeaten egg whites,
1 white of leek,
1 minced red of carrot,

1½ fluid oz wine vinegar,
4 peppercorns,
2 crushed eggshells with inner
  skins removed,
4 fluid oz cooking sherry.

Place stock, prepared beef, leek and carrot in stock pot or roomy pan, bring to boil, skim, level off at simmer, maintain for maximum 2 hours. Strain, return to clean pan, add all remaining ingredients, crushing eggshells first, return pan to moderate heat, watch unceasingly until thick foam forms on top and mixture begins to boil. Draw to edge of heat, reduce heat to minimum and allow to shiver/simmer very gently 30 minutes. Ladle off as much foam as is possible without disturbing liquor beneath. Strain over jelly bag and use.

Note: This may also be made with chicken stock in which case replace beef (steak) with smashed-down boiling fowl; or with veal stock, in which case replace beef with 1 lb lean pie veal. In either case, recipe is then followed through as before.

173 2nd Level Consommé

This is made with absolutely cleared stock which has previously been reduced by vigorous simmering from 3 pints to 1 pint. Then the reduced liquor is placed in a roomy pan with 1 separated unbeaten raw egg white to every pint, 1 torn bay leaf, 2 gills sherry, 2 cloves, 8 peppercorns, 2 crushed egg shells with inner skins removed; 1 dessertspoonful wine vinegar. Put all over a low heat and bring **extremely slowly** to boiling point WHISKING UNCEASINGLY. Slide an asbestos mat over lowest possible heat and allow mixture to shiver/simmer as gently as possible for 30 minutes. By this time a thick head of grubby foam will have formed on top. Below this is the clear consommé. Spoon off as much foam as possible without reaching consommé. Then turn into jelly bag and strain. Let it drip for at least 1 hour. Use clear consommé as desired.

174 Consommé en Gelée (from a tin)

1 tin beef consommé,
scant ¼ oz powdered gelatine,
1 dessertspoonful cooking brandy,
1 tablespoonful cooking-type sherry,
¼ pint clear beef stock,
white pepper,
1 tablespoonful scissored chives.

Place stock in pan. Shake gelatine over surface. Stir in, continue stirring until mixture is completely clear, stir in consommé then brandy and sherry. Season to taste with pepper. Turn into bowl, refrigerate overnight. In morning, whip to a froth with a fork. Pile into small bowls. Refrigerate until service. Scatter chives over each bowl.

Basic Bone Stock

For our favourite basic bone stock, use 2 unsalted pigs' trotters and 6 lb of pork bones. You can also obtain a good stock from the same amount of sawn-down beef bones plus a bouquet garni. There is an excellent one to be obtained from 6 lb lamb bones and 1 lb scrag end of lamb.

Whichever you choose, just turn bones into a roomy container,

124

cover liberally with cold water, bring to boil, skim, refresh with cold water to cover bones by at least 1 inch, re-boil, set at steady simmer and maintain unaided for an absolute minimum 3 hours. Leave until quite cold, remove the fat crust and use.

To last indefinitely: Raise fat-denuded bone stock to boiling point, simmer on for a minimum 20 minutes, daily. Remove to a cold place.

To remove fat from stock instantly: Tow small pieces of tissue paper or absorbent kitchen paper over surface. Either type of paper will gradually absorb the grease and leave a clear liquid for you to draw upon.

Oven Made Stock

Use either large saucepan (without a long handle) or stock pot. If former make "lid" of thick aluminium cooking foil. On stove bring chosen contents to boil, skim, refresh with tumbler cold water. Cover and put into oven 240 F (gas 2), second shelf from bottom for 10 hours. Thus stock can be done overnight or during day. If needed immediately thereafter, skim off top fatty accumulations with towed-over pieces of absorbent kitchen paper. All stock should thereafter be daily re-boiled and then re-simmered minimum 20 minutes to ensure perfect freshness. Thus never add such souring agents as carrots, turnips, potatoes, Jerusalem artichokes or other soil in-bedded items. Onions are alright, they sit on top of soil!

Chicken Stock

(A)
1 boiling fowl,   *4 parsley stalks,*
12 shallots,   *3 quarts water.*

Smash chicken to pulp with a large blunt weapon. We wrap an old flat iron in a tea towel and bash away! Put with neck and giblets in a roomy pan with all remaining ingredients. Bring to the boil, skim carefully, simmer for 2 hours but, do not boil hard please. Strain, return to cleaned pan and simmer on until fluid is reduced to 2 pints. Use as required.

(B)

1 chicken carcase and any	*2 sets giblets,*
available chicken bones,	*4 parsley stalks,*
4 chickens' necks,	*3 quarts water.*

Smash down carcase to force bones to yield up their juices. Meanwhile put all remaining ingredients into roomy pan and simmer for $1\frac{1}{2}$ hours. Add smashed carcase and bones, simmer on for $1\frac{1}{2}$ hours, strain, return to clean pan and simmer on until fluid is reduced to 2 pints.

---

175 Clear Hare Soup

1 freshly killed small hare or	*$\frac{1}{4}$ oz peppercorns,*
leveret,	*4 basil leaves (when available),*
1 lb lean beef,	*3 quarts beef bone stock,*
1 slice raw ham or gammon,	*$\frac{1}{4}$ pint cooking-type port,*
1 faggot herbs,	*salt and pepper.*
1 large, scraped, lengthwise-	
quartered carrot,	

Skin hare, then gut completely, removing liver. Divide into neat pieces. Set in large stock-pot or jam kettle, all ingredients except liver. Bring to boil, skim, level off at steady simmer and maintain for 6 hours. Strain through 2 folds muslin pressed into and over rim of an ordinary sieve. Leave until hare and strained liquor are quite cold. Skim off any residue fat from liquor. Cut $\frac{1}{2}$ lb of hare from fat thighs into matchsticks. Put into soup, bring to the boil and serve with liver croûtons. For these cut $\frac{1}{4}$ inch thick crustless triangles, fry in "singing" butter and oil. Scrape liver on a board. Dissolve 1 oz butter in a small pan, add scraped liver and stir/fry until well coloured. Season lightly with salt and pepper, spread on fried croûtons and hand separately.

176 Brown Soup Stock (Bouillon)

2 lb beef shin,
4 pints water,
4 oz diced carrot,
1 large onion,
4 cloves,
4 oz chopped celery,

4 oz diced turnip,
2 parsley stalks,
4 crushed peppercorns,
2 lb good beef bones,
2 oz dripping.

Rub dripping over bones, bake at 400 F (gas 6), mid-shelf for 20 minutes. Remove bones, place in stock pot with all remaining ingredients except seasonings. Bring to boil, skim, refresh with tumbler cold water, raise to steady simmer and maintain 4 hours. Strain through four folds butter muslin fitted over ordinary sieve, season and serve.

177 Consommé en Gelée

This is lightly set, cold consommé frothed with a fork and piled into well-chilled soup bowls. This is then top sprinkled with finely milled parsley heads.

178 Fake Consommé

When you are desperate, open a large tin consommé, add ½ tin water or cleared stock, 2 fluid oz dry white wine, 1 teaspoonful wine vinegar, generous pinch white pepper. Stir all ingredients over heat until boiling and use with light flavouring of lemon juice.

179 Fake Consommé en Gelée

Add 1 rounded teaspoonful powdered gelatine to Fake Consommé (See above). Stir until clear, allow to set very loosely. For service, froth and serve.

180 The Service of Tinned Turtle Soup

You may be interested to know that in the lesser brands the "turtle" pieces are simmered-until-silky-tender pieces of pig's ears!

1 standard tin turtle soup,
1½ tins clear meat stock,
3 fluid oz sherry,

1 rounded dessertspoonful
milled, fresh parsley heads,
pinch of cayenne pepper.

Mix all together except parsley and raise to boiling point. Stir in parsley and serve with Danish caviare-type (sold in very small pots) spread over stamped out 1½ inch diameter rounds of egg/milk fried croûtons (page 16).

181 Petite Marmite

1 lb neck of very lean beef,
1 lb breast of beef,
1 marrow bone tied in muslin,
6 chicken necks,
6 wing tips,
6 gizzards,
7 pints water,

¾ oz salt,
6 medium cubed carrots,
6 cubed turnips,
5 oz white of leeks, sliced finely,
1 celery heart,
6 oz white cabbage, blanched.

Put both beef pieces cut small with marrow bone, water and salt into large pot or pan. Raise to boiling, skim and simmer 3 hours. Add chicken and vegetables, except cabbage, simmer 1 hour. Add shredded prepared cabbage, cook 5 minutes more and skim. Strain through double muslin over sieve. Return vegetables, bring to boil, correct seasoning, serve with Marrow Toast (page 21).

182 Poule au Pot (Poule au Pot Henri IV)

This is Petite Marmite (see above) into which, for the last hour, a very plump young chicken is poached gently in place of the chicken giblets.

183 Bouillon de Boeuf

1 lb least costly stewing steak,
7 large radishes sliced finely,
1 oz finely-chopped spring onion,
3 oz diced green or red
* pimento,*

2 oz thinly-sliced onion,
4 pints beef bone stock,
salt and pepper,
1 bouquet garni,
2 oz dripping.

Heat dripping. When "singing" turn in matchstick-cut steak and turn/fry briskly to seal. Drain, put in casserole and fry vegetables in pan residue. Turn occasionally until well impregnated, add to casserole with all remaining ingredients except seasonings. Cover and cook on centre shelf 335 F (gas 3) for 3 hours or overnight 11 p.m. to 8 a.m. 240 F (gas ¼) lowest shelf. Chill, remove fatty surface and fish out herbs. Re-heat, taste, correct seasoning.

Note: Dice of bread may be fried in skimmed-off fat until browned and handed separately.

184 Bouillon Czarina

3 pints chicken stock A,
* (page 125),*
2 oz sultanas,
1 oz finely chopped fresh
* tarragon leaves,*

3 oz hair-thin strips lean
* cooked ham,*
1 oz sliced stuffed olives
* (with pimentoes),*
1 oz sliced unskinned
* mushrooms.*

Clear stock thoroughly, place in pan with all remaining ingredients except sultanas. Pour boiling water over sultanas in small container and leave 10 minutes. Strain, stir into soup and when piping hot, serve with Garlic Bread (page 13) or fried croûtons.

185 Bouillon Ferneuse

6 round, young turnips,
1 oz butter,
1 oz oil,
4 oz rice,

3 pints·cleared, well-reduced
    chicken or pork stock,
1 oz extra butter,
pinch cayenne.

Chop turnips finely. Heat butter and oil. When "singing" stir in turnips, cover and shake occasionally, cooking over low heat for 15 minutes. Add boiling chosen liquor, stir and when bubbling, add rice. Simmer very gently for 1 hour. Emulsify or sieve, stir in extra butter, taste, correct seasoning and finally add cayenne.

186 Zuppa Pavese (Eggs in clear broth or consommé)

2½ pints clear, strongly reduced
    chicken, meat or vegetable
    stock,
6 eggs,

18 small squares bread,
grated Parmesan cheese or
    substitute hard cheese.

Having reduced the chosen stock until it REALLY TASTES and while it is hot, poach eggs in it, in wide shallow pan. Lift out into heated soup bowls, pour stock over until filled, using strainer if you have any thread of egg white floating about in stock. Fry bread, spread grated cheese liberally over each, float three around each egg in each bowl. Hand extra cheese separately.

Note: This is marvellous for someone who lives alone as well as for a large family, except that the live-aloner might be compelled to use a small tin of consommé suitably diluted with tap water! When making for 6 people as given in our recipe, please bear one thing in mind. If you use tap water instead of reduced stock or if you use a bouillon cube, that is what it will taste like! The better the stock, the better the soup . . . and the better for YOU!

187 Consommé aux Tomates

2½ pints real consommé
  (page 123),
1 lb very ripe skinned, de-seeded
  tomatoes,
2 fresh basil leaves or 1 flat
  teaspoonful powdered dried
  basil,

salt and pepper,
celery salt,
2 tablespoonsful cooking
  sherry.

Rough cut tomatoes, place in small, thick pan with 1 pint consommé, simmer very gently with basil 20 minutes. Rub through sieve, leave in bowl to settle. Then pour all but base sediment into pan with bulk of consommé. Taste, correct seasoning and simmer down to 1½ pints. Stir in sherry and serve.

188 Consommé de Laitues

2 well-washed Cos lettuces,
6 crisp beetroot leaves,
1 small fistful de-stemmed
  sorrel leaves,
the white of 2 fat leeks sliced
  finely,
3 large or 8 slim spring carrots,
1 large or 2 small peeled garlic
  cloves,

salt and pepper,
1 rounded teaspoonful castor
  sugar,
cleared, well reduced stock or
  consommé,
1 slice brown bread per head,
1 egg yolk,
generous pinch chervil.

Chop all vegetables finely, crush garlic, toss all into boiling chosen liquor with stock to cover and sugar. Boil, skim, simmer 35 minutes. Remove from heat, beat egg yolk, pour on a little soup, beat, return to pan, stir quickly, correct seasoning and place small piece brown toast in base of each bowl. Pour soup over.

189 Consommé Colnet

1 quart chicken consommé   3 oz chopped white of celery,
   (page 147),   2 oz butter.
3 oz chopped red of carrots,

Soften butter over lowest possible heat. Add carrots and celery and cook with extreme gentleness until collapsed and very soft. Stir into hot consommé and run absorbent kitchen paper over top surface to remove any butter spots.

190 Consommé à la Colbert

1½ pints chicken consommé   1 tablespoonful shelled peas,
   (page 147),   1 tablespoonful chopped spring
4 smallest eggs,   onions,
1 tablespoonful chopped baby   2 tablespoonsful wine vinegar.
   carrots,

Heat consommé, steam vegetables then raise consommé to boiling point. Half fill a frying pan with hot water. Stir in vinegar, slip asbestos mat between pan and low flame. Slide in eggs broken into a saucer singly. Flip vinegar water over them. On no account allow heat to rise. When tops are white-veiled, pour soup into four heated soup bowls. Slice 1 poached egg into each and serve fast.

191 Consommé au Cresson Alenois

2¼ pints beef consommé   boiling salted water.
   (page 123),
1 large bunch fresh watercress
   picked and de-leafed,

Bring consommé to boiling point while lowering watercress leaves into salted boiling water in a small pan. Give 1 minute, turn into strainer, pass cress under cold running water to refresh, wipe and turn on to consommé. Simmer 1 minute longer.

192 Consommé de Volaille aux Diablotins

This is chicken consommé (page 147), poured into heated bowls and 2 or 3 Diablotins (page 12) floated on top of each.

193 Consommé à la Bourgeoise

1 quart beef consommé
  (page 123),
5 extra fluid oz consommé,
1 medium carrot,

2 shallots,
1 small turnip,
1 medium onion, all diced small,
1 generous pinch chervil.

Simmer vegetables in extra consommé until the latter is syrupy. Stir into heated consommé and serve.

194 Consommé Brillat-Savarin

1 quart chicken consommé
  (page 147),
2 oz medium tapioca,
2 rounded tablespoonsful cooked
  chicken meat cut into
  matchsticks,

1 small, paper-thin pancake
  rolled and cut into hair-strips,
4 outside Cos lettuce leaves
  shredded finely,
2 sorrel leaves shredded finely.

Heat consommé, poach tapioca in it gently for 10 minutes. Add all remaining ingredients and poach on for 10 minutes more.

195 Consommé Chasseur

1 quart game consommé
  (page 147),
2 rounded tablespoonsful
  minutely sliced unskinned
  mushrooms,

1½ fluid oz dry Madeira,
1 eggspoonful chervil leaves
  chopped small.

Heat consommé, add mushrooms and chervil, poach 5 minutes over low heat. Add Madeira, just allow to regain heat then serve.

196 Consommé à la Chilienne

1 quart chicken consommé
  (page 147),
2 oz rice,

1 tablespoonful diced, skinned
  red pimento,
1 eggspoonful finely chopped
  chervil.

Heat consommé, toss in rice, simmer very gently 15 minutes, adding pimento dice after 10 minutes. Stir in chervil and serve.

197 Consommé aux Piments Doux

1 quart chicken consommé
  (page 147),

1 red pimento, de-pipped,
  pithed and diced small.

Simmer both ingredients together for 10 minutes and serve.

198 Consommé à la Portugaise

1 quart real consommé
  (page 123),
6 fluid oz fresh tomato purée,

6 fluid oz fresh tomato juice,
cayenne pepper.

Poach both tomato ingredients with consommé for 20 minutes over lowest possible heat. Stir in good pinch cayenne and serve.

199 Consommé de Volaille Napolitaine

Proceed exactly as for Consommé à la Portugaise (see above) using chicken consommé (page 147). When soup is completed stir in either 1 port glassful of modest port, or the same of old Marsala.

200 Consommé Brancas

1 quart beef consommé
  (page 123),
1 small washed Cos lettuce
  rolled and sliced extremely
  thinly,
2 rounded tablespoonfuls
  crumbled vermicelli,
10 fluid oz ($\frac{1}{2}$ pt) extra consommé,

1 oz butter,
2 tablespoonsful finely sliced,
  unskinned mushrooms,
1 heaped tablespoonful dice of
  potatoes,
1 generous pinch chervil.

Toss chervil and lettuce into hot consommé and simmer 2 minutes. Remove from heat while frying mushrooms in given butter and poaching potatoes and vermicelli in extra consommé until tender. Add to main bulk, re-boil and serve.

201 Minestra Mille Fanti

2 oz freshly crumbled bread
  rubbed through sieve,
3 oz grated Parmesan cheese,
nutmeg,

salt and pepper,
2 eggs,
1$\frac{1}{2}$ pints consommé.

Bring consommé to boil, draw to edge of low heat. Mix cheese and fine crumbs in bowl, beat well with a wooden spoon, adding eggs singly. Turn mixture over hot consommé, stir again, then leave on edge of heat turning pan round at intervals for overall 15 minutes. Taste, correct seasoning add nutmeg to taste, then whisk up vigorously and serve at once. NEVER ALLOW TO BOIL.

202 Consommé aux Trois Filets

1 quart chosen consommé,

1 rounded tablespoonful cooked
  chicken, cooked tongue and
  cooked mushrooms cut into
  matchsticks.

Slide these three into consommé, simmer for 2 minutes and serve.

203 Consommé aux Profiteroles

For convenience and economy, this consommé should be served
when a batch of water choux paste for some other items can be
borrowed from. Put 2 tablespoonsful of choux paste into a small
paper icing bag with ⅛ inch diameter plain writing pipe affixed.
Have 1 quart of consommé boiling and set at steady simmer. Hold
pipe and bag horizontally across soup surface and lop off minute
lengths with wetted knife, letting them fall into soup. Cook until
puffy—about 2 minutes. Ladle consommé and profiterolles into
heated bowl. Serve immediately.

204 Consommé au Parmesan

1 quart chosen consommé,   *Garniture Parmesan.*

Work together 2 egg yolks, pinch salt and pepper and 1½ oz real
Parmesan. Work 2 rounded soupspoonsful sifted flour into 2 very
stiffly beaten egg whites. Cut gently into egg yolk batter. Spread
over liberally buttered wax paper as thinly as possible on a flat
baking sheet. Cook at 425 F (gas 7) 1 shelf above centre for 4–5
minutes. Remove, cool and stamp into tiny rounds of fancy shapes.
At moment of service slide 1 dessertspoonful over each bowl of
consommé.

205 Consommé à la Royale de Tomate

The quick way to this soup is to make the Royale as given in
Consommé à la Royale (page 138), beating in with given eggs, 1 flat
dessertspoonful concentrated tomato purée. Otherwise continue
exactly as given for previous soup.

206 Consommé à la Royale d'Epinards

2 rounded tablespoonsful spinach   *pinch salt and pepper,*
  purée,   *1 standard egg.*
2 tablespoonsful thick Béchamel,

136

Beat egg thoroughly into Béchamel, add spinach, beat again. Turn into small, shallow buttered container. Stand in outer 1 inch boiling water and poach under foil or paper covering until just set. Treat as for Consommé à la Royale (page 138) using 1 quart any chosen consommé as indicated therein.

207 Consommé Xavier

This is chicken, beef or game consommé into which a pinch of chopped chervil, a pinch of salt and a teaspoonful finely-chopped fresh parsley is stirred at moment of service. Immediately prior to service, stir in dry sherry to taste—it is not fair to be arbitrary about the quantity.

208 Consommé à la Madrilene

1 quart consommé which sets to
light jelly when cold,
2 medium tomatoes,

pinch cayenne,
pinch paprika.

Peel tomatoes, halve, remove all pips and centre core, chop neatly. Fork up soup-jelly into a light froth, fork in all given ingredients, pile into chilled soup bowls or glasses.

209 Consommé à l'Aurore

2½ pints consommé (page 123),
1½ oz large tapioca,
1½ oz diced, cooked, French
beans,

Royale (page 138),
1 tablespoonful sieved, cooked
spinach,
1 raw egg white.

Poach tapioca in 2 pints consommé for 12 minutes. Make Royale, fold in spinach. Cook as for Royale. Cool, turn on to table and chop finely. When tapioca is cooked, stir in prepared French beans, spinach Royale and egg white, poached until set, then chopped.

210 Consommé Glacé à l'Estragon

Take chosen consommé to clarification stage. After straining, simmer down to 1 quart with 2 finely chopped 2 inch heads fresh tarragon (French). Then clarify, chill to ensure consommé sets to a light jelly. Add an extra pinch finely chopped fresh tarragon to top of each serving.

211 Consommé à la Parisienne

1 quart chicken consommé
  (page 147),
2 oz diced carrots,
2 oz diced potatoes,
2 oz diced French beans,
1 oz diced turnip,
10 extra fluid oz chicken
  consommé.

Place prepared vegetables and extra consommé in pan and simmer until vegetables are tender and liquor is syrupy. Stir into main bulk consommé, add 1 mean flat teaspoonful chopped chervil whenever possible.

212 Consommé à la Royale

1 quart chicken, beef or game
  consommé,
3 standard eggs,
pinch salt,
pinch pepper,
7 fluid oz extra consommé.

Royale is a garnish "suffix". To make, beat up whole eggs with salt and pepper, beat in extra consommé gradually, turn into lightly buttered mould. Stand in outer pan of water coming 1 inch up mould. Cover with piece of wax paper, simmer until just set, chill, run knife round edge, turn out. Either stamp with tiny garnish cutters into little stars, crescents etc., or just dice. When chosen consommé is boiling pour into heated soup bowls, add 1 dessert-spoonful of Royale to each portion.

213 Consommé de Poisson

(This is a most subtle and elegant dinner-party brew.)

138

3 large minced carrots,
4 large diced onions,
3 large outside sliced stick
  celery,
4 diced shallots,
1 crushed garlic clove,
3 cloves,
2 medium bay leaves,
1 sprig thyme,
12 parsley stalks,
10 pints cold water,

1 pint white Bordeaux,
1½ oz sea or Maldon salt,
2 crushed black peppercorns,
2 lb gurnet, cut into small pieces
  on bone,
6 small whiting,
2 raw egg whites,
2 skinless egg shells,
2 oz butter,
2 fluid oz oil.

Remove fillets from whiting and set aside. Heat oil with dissolved butter in large frying pan and turn in prepared vegetables. Cook gently, turning occasionally until collapsed and tender, turn into large pot or pan. Add water, salt, peppercorns, herbs, garlic, gurnet, remains of whiting, then bring to boil, skim, simmer for 1¾ hours. Add wine, simmer on for 20 minutes. Strain thoroughly through 2 folds muslin in fine sieve. Turn into clean pan, add pounded whiting fillets, crushed eggshells, unbeaten egg whites. Whip unceasingly over low heat until mixture boils and thick, scummy foam forms on top. Stop whipping. Draw to side of burner, leave to simmer for 30 minutes. Strain through a jelly bag. Simmer down to a mere 3½ pints.

---

214 Consommé Kandourow

1 quart chicken consommé
  (page 147),
¼ pint stiffly whipped double
  cream,
2 stiffly-whipped egg whites,

salt and pepper,
½ oz finely grated Parmesan
  cheese.

Have consommé piping hot. Blend cream into egg whites, add cheese, salt and pepper to taste. Turn in onto consommé in pan, smooth off neatly, draw pan to side of lowest flame and leave 30 minutes. Then, ladling from base to pick up soup, ladle into soup bowls which should have consommé in each one totally masked by a dome of foam.

215 Consommé de Poisson Normande

*1 quart Consommé de Poisson
  (page 138),
1 pint steamed mussels,
¼ pint shelled shrimps,
1 cleaned diced large scallop,*

*1 oz butter,
1 heaped dessertspoonful milled
  parsley heads,
Diablotins (page 12),*

Poach diced scallop in hot melted butter until stiffened and free of opaque appearance. Strain, add to consommé with mussels removed from shell, shrimps and parsley. Ladle into heated soup bowls. Float 2 or 3 Diablotins on top of each at moment of service.

216 Consommé de Poisson aux Crevettes

*Consommé de Poisson
  (page 138),
¼ pint shelled shrimps,*

*1 rounded tablespoonful fresh,
  milled parsley heads.*

Pour boiling consommé into heated bowls. Divide shrimps between portions, scatter parsley over top of each serving.

217 Consommé Hollandaise

*1 flat dessertspoonful paprika
  powder,
2 rounded tablespoonsful
  chickens' liver quenelles,*

*2 rounded tablespoonsful beef-
  bone marrow,
1 quart beef consommé
  (page 123).*

Toss paprika into soup. Make baby quenelles with 2 oz chicken livers, 1 small raw egg white, 1 oz crumb of bread passed through milk until collapsed. Squeeze wet bread in clean cloth. Pound scraped livers in mortar with pestle adding crumb gradually, then sufficient egg-white to make **very** firm, just-too-stiff-to-pipe paste. Finally stir in a few drops double cream. Pound and pound relentlessly, turn into nylon icing bag with ¼ inch plain writing pipe affixed. As soup bubbles, hold bag horizontally over and with knife dipped constantly into cold water squeeze and lop off minute "corks" into bubbling mixture below. They sink! When risen again, soup is ready to serve with dice of marrow bone stirred in at the last. One hour before, tie marrow bone in clean cloth, immerse in boiling water, simmer 1 hour. Cool, unwrap, scoop out marrow, cut into dice to await last minute immersing into consommé. Optionally garnish with scattered chervil leaves chopped finely.

218 Consommé d'Homard

Drip 2 or 3 small medallions cut from saddle of cooked lobster into each bowlful of Consommé de Poisson (page 138). Pipe a blob of stiffly whipped cream into the centre of each bowlful at moment of service. Optionally scatter cream with tiny pinches of finely chopped fennel.

219 Consommé aux Moules

1 quart Consommé d'Homard (see above),

1½ pints mussels in shell.

Steam scrubbed, bearded mussels for 3 minutes. Remove mussels from open shells. Discard closed ones. Bring soup to boil. Stir in mussels and serve.

220 Consommé à l'Orge du Perles

1 quart beef consommé (page 123) in which 3 oz pearl barley has been poached for 10 minutes immediately prior to service. Serve with Diablotins (page 12).

221 Consommé à la Florentine

1½ pints chicken consommé (page 147),
1 smallest egg,

extra 5 fluid ozs (¼ pint) chicken consommé (page 147), simmered 10 minutes with 1 teaspoonful rice.

Beat egg lightly with fork. Hold small sieve over the just-simmering consommé. Dribble egg into sieve. Stir consommé meanwhile with a fork to make egg form itself into those strands which you may have drunk already in soups when in Chinese restaurants. Carefully add consommé with rice and serve at once.

222 Consommé Florette

2 oz rice,
2½ pints chicken consommé
  (page 147),
2 oz medium tapioca,

salt and pepper,
the white of two medium leeks,
  sliced very thinly,
2 oz butter.

Simmer tapioca, rice and consommé together for 15 minutes. Soften butter in small pan, stir in leeks and cook with extreme gentleness until these collapse and are extremely tender. Stir into consommé. Run a piece of absorbent kitchen paper over top-surface to remove any butter spots, season and serve.

223 Consommé aux Gombos à l'Orientale

2¼ pints chosen consommé,
2 oz rice,

generous pinch cayenne pepper,
4 oz well-rinsed tinned gombos.

Slice gombos into little rounds. Simmer rice in consommé for 15 minutes. Add gombos and cayenne. Hand 3½ inch diameter pancakes rolled over paprika butter (page 21) with lengthwise split gombos in each.

224 Consommé au Macaroni

either 1 quart beef consommé or
  well-reduced beef bone stock,

4 oz broken macaroni,
1 quart salted boiling water.

Toss macaroni into boiling salted water. Maintain at bubbling boil for 8 minutes. Strain, add to stock or consommé and simmer on for further 10 minutes. Ideally hand grated hard cheese separately.

225 Consommé Mercedes

1 quart chicken consommé
  (page 147),
2 fluid oz sherry,
1 pinch cayenne pepper,

2 oz chickens' kidneys sliced
  thinly,
1 mean teaspoonful chopped
  chervil,
salt and pepper.

Simmer consommé with chickens' kidneys for 10 minutes. Add cayenne and chervil, taste, add salt and pepper as desired. Stir in sherry and simmer on for 3 minutes.

226 Consommé de Racines Fraiches

1 lb carrots cut into matchsticks,
1 lb diced onions,
1 bouquet garni,
3 oz dripping or 1½ oz butter
  and 1½ oz oil,
1 lb ordinary peas,
1 lb small, white, dried beans
  overnight-soaked,

2 thinly-sliced Cos lettuces,
6 pints carefully cleared,
  strongly reduced bone stock,
1¼ oz salt,
mean 1½ oz black peppercorns,
1 pinch cinnamon,
3 cloves,
2 sticks chopped celery.

Dissolve and heat chosen fats in frying pan. Turn in carrots and onions, fry gently until soft but not browned. Turn into large pot or pan, add all remaining ingredients, bring to boil, skim, simmer extremely gently 3 hours. Strain, remove herbs, re-heat and serve in large tureen with heated dish containing mixed vegetables. Hand separate bowl of fried croûtons (page 17) or Diablotins (page 12).

227 Consommé Julienne

the red of 4 medium carrots cut
  into matchsticks,
4 medium whole carrots cut into
  matchsticks,
1 medium celery heart cut into
  matchsticks,
3 medium onions cut into
  matchsticks,

6 cleaned, trimmed, medium
  leeks cut into matchsticks,
3 oz fine-diced, raw, unsalted
  pork fat,
6 pints beef consommé,
1 teaspoonful castor sugar.

Fry pork dice over brisk heat in large frying pan until fat runs freely and dice shrivel. Strain, return to pan, add all vegetable matchsticks and fry 3 minutes. Turn into roomy pot or pan. Add consommé, simmer over lowest possible heat for 3 hours. Skim, draw pieces of absorbent kitchen paper over top-surface to clear off all grease, add sugar and serve.

228 Pot-au-Feu à la Languedocienne

Pot-au-Feu

one 6 inch by 12 inch (or
  equivalent) piece of raw,
  unsalted pork fat on rind.

Blanch the pork fat by pouring boiling water over it and leaving 4 minutes. Take out and when cool enough to handle, roll up and tie with fine string. Immerse in the pot during main cooking time. This imparts a unique flavour to a Pot-au-Feu.

Pot au Feu: Put 10 oz beef flank, 8 oz beef bones and $3\frac{1}{4}$ pints of cold water into a stock-pot. Bring to boil, skim, pour on a further $\frac{1}{2}$ pint cold water, re-boil and simmer for $\frac{3}{4}$ hour. Add $\frac{1}{2}$ oz salt, 3 peppercorns, 1 small head celery, 1 turnip, 1 carrot, 1 sprig chervil, 1 bay leaf, $\frac{1}{2}$ leek split downwards, 1 small parsnip, 1 small onion stuck with 2 cloves and slightly browned in a little very hot dripping, 1 small well-washed lettuce, 1 garlic clove and $\frac{1}{2}$ a small firm cabbage heart previously blanched and tied up with fine string. Replace lid, regain boiling point, adjust heat to steady simmer and continue until vegetables are tender. Strain.

Place meat in a large soup tureen, skim fat from liquor and re-boil it. Either pour over the contents of the tureen or serve in a jug putting some meat and vegetables in each person's bowl and filling up with the soup. Serve with rounds of French bread baked until pale golden.

229 Consommé Hudson

1 quart Consommé de Poisson (page 138),
3 medium, slightly over-ripe tomatoes,

1 oz butter,
2 oz flaked, white crab meat,
2 oz matchstick cut, skinned, cucumber.

Melt butter, add skinned, de-pipped tomato flesh, simmer until soft and collapsed. Sieve into consommé, add crab meat and cucumber, simmer 3 minutes and serve.

230 Curry and Apple Soup

1½ oz pork, chicken fat or very clean dripping,
1 large onion chopped small,
1 generously rounded teaspoonful Masala paste,
1¼ pints chicken stock (A or B page 125),

1 oz flour,
2 fairly large, sweet apples, peeled and cored,
the strained juice of ½ lemon,
a few watercress leaves,
salt and pepper.

Dissolve chosen fat. When it "sings" slide in onions and cook until tender but not browned. Work in flour and Masala with back of wooden spoon until soft ball forms. Dilute with gradual additions of chicken stock, beating well between each addition until all is absorbed. Taste, correct flavour with salt and pepper. Cut all flesh from apple core. Dice very finely, cover with lemon juice. Leave until moment of service. Then stir into hot soup, pour into heated bowls and scatter watercress leaves over each serving.

231 Consommé de Concombre (Cold Cucumber Soup)

Probably the easiest to make on record!

*1 medium-sized hot-house
  cucumber,
1 large shallot,
strained juice of 1 medium lemon,
¾ pint good clear white stock,
1 flat dessertspoonful gelatine,
salt and pepper,*

*1 teaspoonful finely chopped
  fresh mint,
2 tablespoonsful dry white wine
  (can be omitted),
2 tablespoonsful hot water,
1 pint milk.*

Grate cucumber with skin still on. Grate peeled shallot. Dissolve gelatine in hot water. Strain, blend all together. Add milk. Correct seasoning. Chill and serve.

Note: It is unnecessary, but we do serve this cold soup with a small decoration of whole shelled shrimps floated on top in a star design, when using for dinner parties.

232 Consommé au Fumet des Fines Herbes

*2½ pints beef consommé
8 tomatoes,
1 saltspoonful finely chopped
  tarragon,
1 saltspoonful finely chopped
  parsley.*

*1 saltspoonful finely chopped
  thyme,
1 saltspoonful finely chopped
  chervil,
salt and pepper.*

Dice the de-seeded, skinned tomato flesh very neatly and emulsify with 2 fluid oz consommé. Stir into remainder of consommé, raise to boiling point, simmer 4 minutes. Meanwhile pound all four herbs really viciously in a mortar with a pestle. Stir into simmering soup. Simmer 2 minutes more and hand a little bowl of grated cheese separately for each person to stir into soup. Very refreshing to the palate.

233 Cornish Kiddley Broth

twelve 2 inch squares thin bread, 1 oz butter,
6 marigold heads, salt and pepper,
2 tablespoonsful scissored chives, very strong bone stock.

Place stock in pan, boil, add marigold heads, chives, butter and season to taste. Simmer 10 minutes. Strain over bread squares in soup bowl and serve with "Tiddely Pasties" (page 20).

234 Game Consommé

4 lb fresh game bones and 2 oz butter,
   carcases 1 oz olive oil,
1 small turnip, diced small, 1 large carrot,
1 finely sliced white and green 1 bouquet garni,
   of leek, 2 mushrooms (flat),
1 stick chopped celery, 2 black peppercorns,
cold water, 4 white peppercorns.

Dissolve butter in largest frying pan, heat with oil, then reduce flame to low and turn in all vegetables. Cover, shake frequently and fry 20 minutes. Put bones and carcases into large pot or pan, add fried and all other remaining ingredients. Cover liberally with cold water, raise to boil, skim and simmer gently for $2\frac{1}{2}$–3 hours. Strain through muslin over sieve. Reduce liquor by simmering to 3 pints then follow instructions for final stage (adding 1 lb raw, minced rabbit or hare) from 2nd Level Consommé (page 124).

235 Chicken Consommé

Stage 1 Make basic liquor as for Real Consommé (page 123) substituting chicken bones for beef bones, otherwise copy instructions for Real Consommé.

Stage 2 When simmered, liquor is strained and returned to pot or pan, add viciously smashed-down carcase of one boiling fowl instead of minced beef in Real Consommé and then follow instructions.

236 Consommé Vert Pré

1 quart chicken consommé
  (page 147),
2 tablespoonsful coarse tapioca,
1 tablespoonful asparagus tips,
1 tablespoonful peas,

1 tablespoonful French beans,
  diced,
1 fat roll of lettuce leaves sliced
  very finely,
a little extra consommé.

Poach lettuce and all vegetables in extra consommé until tender and liquor syrupy. Simmer boiling consommé with tapioca 15 minutes, mix both together. Pour into tureen for family service.

237 Consommé à l'Essence de Celeri

1 quart chosen consommé,
  beef, game or chicken,

2 well-washed outer stems and
  hearts of celery chopped small.

Place both together in roomy pan. Simmer with extreme gentleness for 45 minutes. Strain and scatter a few celery pieces over each filled bowl.

Soups From Other Lands

238. Caldo Verde
239. Touring à l'Oignon
240. Touring Blanchi
241. Garlic Soup for Cold Sufferers
242. Vichyssoise
243. Soupe Chasseur
244. Berliner Erbsensuppe
245. Spargelsuppe
246. Soupe au Choux
247. Paparot
248. Ukranian Bortsch
249. Kartoffelsuppe
250. Soupe aux Tomates Provençale
251. Minestrone
252. Andalusian Soup
253. Kalsoppe mit Frikadeller
254. Grauwe Erwertensuppe
255. Soup au Pistou
256. Gulasleves
257. Nettle Soup
258. Creole Corn Soup
259. Crème de Navettes
260. Soupe de la Nuit de Noce
261. French Nursery Soup
262. Peruvian Avocado
263. Dutch Tomato Soup
264. Pomidorova Zupa
265. Purée de Choux de Bruxelles
266. Cerbah
267. Soupe à l'Oignon Oporto
268. Soupe Polonaise
269. Soupe Savoyarde

238 Caldo Verde (Portuguese Potato and Cabbage Soup)

1 lb old, peeled potatoes,
1 medium grated raw onion,
salt and pepper,
2 pints chicken stock (A or B,
  (page 125),

2 breakfastcupfuls raw sliced
  cabbage,
1 tablespoonful olive oil.

The whole secret of this excellent, simple soup is in the cutting of the cabbage which must be in the finest, most delicate hair-thin strips. The rest is simple! Rough-cut potatoes, cook until soft in stock, sieve, return to pan, correct seasoning and 3 minutes before serving toss in cabbage shreds, cover and simmer **hard** for 3 minutes with olive oil; correct seasoning and serve.

239 Touring à l'Oignon

10 oz chopped onions,
1 oz flour,
2 oz pork or goose fat,
2 oz melting-type cheese
  (ideally Gruyère),

4½ pints good bone stock,
salt and pepper,
4 thin slices sandwich-loaf
  bread.

Mince chopped onions finely, heat chosen fat. When "singing", fry onions until very soft. Scatter flour over, work in with back of wooden spoon and work in a little stock till a smooth paste is achieved. Add a little more and blend in thoroughly, repeat twice more. Then bring bulk liquor to boiling point, stir in pan paste, simmer steadily for 20 minutes, season to taste. Lay bread slices on ordinary baking sheet. Scatter cheese over them. Cook 355 F (gas 4) mid-shelf for 10 minutes. Cut into small squares, place 2 or 3 in base of each heated soup bowl. Pour soup over and serve.

240 Touring Bianchi (A French peasant garlic soup)

10 oz peeled garlic cloves,
1 large sprig thyme,
1 egg yolk,
1 tablespoonful wine vinegar,
6 very thin slices from a
  sandwich loaf,

salt and pepper,
2 oz pork or goose fat
  (rendered down),
3 pints strong white bone
  stock.

Crush all garlic cloves, fry in hot chosen fat very gently for 4 minutes in a roomy pan. Add thyme, stock, 1 flat teaspoonful salt, ½ flat teaspoonful pepper. Raise to boiling, simmer 10 minutes. Sieve, emulsify or liquidise. Return to pan, stand on asbestos mat over lowest heat. Stir egg yolk with vinegar, stir, little by little into soup. Continue stirring until soup is really hot but not boiling! Cut bread into small strips. Divide between 6 bowls. Pour on soup, removing thyme.

241 Garlic Soup for Cold Sufferers

6 slices quartered bread,
4 peeled garlic cloves,
2 quarts strongly-reduced beef
   stock,

1 fluid oz olive oil,
6 lightly-poached eggs,
salt and pepper,
1 bouquet garni.

Place bread on baking sheet in oven 310 F (gas 2), lowest shelf. Heat oil in tiny pan, fry halved garlic cloves until browned all over. Turn into pan with stock and herbs. Simmer extremely gently 30 minutes. Strain, season, discard garlic and herbs. Place oven-baked bread in each of six wide soup bowls. Slide a poached egg on to each. Ladle soup around gently to fill. Serve instantly.

242 Vichyssoise (Leek and Potato Soup)

2 lb trimmed leeks,
2 lb peeled potatoes,
strong cleared stock,
1–1½ pints milk,

½ pint (ideally) double cream,
salt and pepper,
chopped chives or spring onion
   heads.

Put finely sliced leeks and rough-cut potatoes in a roomy thick pan and cover liberally with stock. Simmer steadily until very tender, sieve, return to clean pan. Add milk, then cream. The amount of milk DOES depend on the consistency you want, but soup should be fairly thick. Season to taste. Serve either icy cold or very hot. Sprinkle each serving with chopped chives; if not available, use finely cut strips of spring onion scissored very small thereafter.

243 Soupe Chasseur

6 finely chopped medium
    mushroom cups,
2 oz butter,
$\frac{1}{2}$ oz oil,
1 coffeespoonful minute chopped
    shallot,
6 fluid oz dry, cooking white
    wine,

1 to 2 tablespoonsful cooking
    brandy,
4 pints beef stock,
$\frac{1}{4}$ pint Tomato Coulis
    (page 34),
1 tablespoonful finely milled
    parsley,
salt and pepper.

Set stock in a pan and allow to bubble until reduced to 1 pint. Dissolve butter, heat with oil and fry shallot gently for 4 minutes. Add mushrooms and fry on until collapsed, add wine and brandy, blend well. Simmer 5 minutes, stir in reduced stock, simmer again 5 minutes, finally add coulis, taste, correct seasoning, serve in heated bowls, sprinkling parsley over each serving.

244 Berliner Erbsensuppe (Berlin Pea Soup)

1 fairly large, chopped onion,
7 oz chopped old potatoes,
1 well-scrubbed pig's ear,
10 oz overnight-soaked, split
    dried peas,
1 bouquet garni,
2 pints cold water,

1 sprig fresh or 1 teaspoonful
    dried marjoram,
2 small, torn bay leaves,
$3\frac{1}{2}$ pints bone stock,
1 rounded tablespoonful fresh
    milled parsley,
salt and pepper,
2 peppercorns.

Stir 1 tablespoonful salt into cold water, bring to boil, immerse ear and simmer 10 minutes. Strain, discard water, place ear in roomy pan with peas, onion, herbs, peppercorns, stock and bouquet garni. Bring to boil, simmer gently for 1$\frac{1}{2}$ hours. Add marjoram, bay leaves, simmer for further 25 minutes. Dredge up ear. Remove all gristle and bone. Dice remainder, return to pot, taste, remove all herbs and correct seasoning. Sprinkle some parsley over each bowlful. Optionally but classically, hand toasted black bread, cubed.

245 Spargelsuppe (German Asparagus Soup)

This is excellent made with sprew (thin, young shoots). German asparagus is white and comparatively tasteless.

1 lb sprew,
2 pints chicken stock (A or B, page 000),
1 separated egg yolk,
2 oz butter,
2 oz sifted flour,

$\frac{1}{2}$ pint milk or top-of-milk or 5 fluid oz of either plus 5 fluid oz single cream,
salt and pepper,
1 flat teaspoonful castor sugar,
pinch nutmeg.

Wash sprew, chop off little heads, set aside; rough chop stalks, simmer in stock with sugar and pinch salt. When tender strain, rub through sieve into stock add milk re-heat. When boiling add butter worked with flour and rolled into tiny balls. Stir in. Beat yolk with top-of-milk or cream, take 1 cupful stock mixture and poach heads very gently. Strain, set aside, return liquor to pan. Stand pan over outer container of hot water, pour on egg/cream mixture, stir until really hot, taste, correct seasoning, float a few sprew heads over each serving.

246 Soupe au Choux

$1\frac{1}{2}$ lb tight white cabbage,
2 oz topped, tailed French beans,
$\frac{1}{4}$ lb shallots or small onions,
2 oz dripping,
1 crushed garlic clove,

4 oz diced streaky bacon,
$2\frac{1}{2}$ pints well-reduced bone stock,
grated hard cheese,
sliced "flute" of French bread,
salt and pepper.

Soften dripping, slice shallots, add with prepared garlic and bacon. Cook gently until shallots are soft but not browned. Turn into roomy pan, add blanched, very thinly sliced cabbage with centre stem grated coarsely. Cover with stock, raise to boiling point, skim, steady off at simmer for 35 minutes, or cook in lidded casserole, low oven shelf for approximately 1 hour, 335 F (gas 3). Add beans, cook on either way until tender. Slice bread into thin rounds. Dry out on bottom oven shelf. During last 30 minutes of cooking time, correct seasoning. For service, float bread on top of pot, serve from pot or in tureen. Sprinkle cheese lightly overall.

247 Paparot (Spinach Soup)

1 lb (picked weight) well-washed and drained fresh spinach,
2½ oz butter,
1 large peeled, crushed garlic clove,
1 generous pinch nutmeg,
salt and pepper,

2 rounded tablespoonsful semolina,
1 heaped tablespoonful flour,
2½ pints water,
½ pint milk,
grated Parmesan cheese.

Place drained spinach with ½ oz butter in thick pan over low heat. Stir occasionally until spinach subsides, cook maximum 7 minutes. Dissolve remaining butter in roomy pan, add flour and garlic, stir to soft ball with 1 flat eggspoonful pepper. Work in water gradually with wooden spoon, allow to come to boil, maintain 3 minutes, work in semolina, sprinkling over surface and stir in. Cook 30 minutes on moderate heat, with occasional stir. Add spinach, sieve, emulsify or liquidise, stir until boiling, taste, correct seasoning, add nutmeg and serve, handing grated cheese separately.

248 Ukranian Bortsch

3 large raw beetroots, peeled and coarse-grated,
1 large onion, coarse-grated,
1 quart beef bone stock

2 oz castor sugar,
salt and pepper,
2 standard eggs,
½ pint soured cream,
strained juice of 2 lemons.

Put prepared beetroots and onions into stock and simmer 35 minutes. Stir in sugar, correct seasoning, simmer on for 5 minutes. Meanwhile whip eggs, whip in cream, beat slowly into soup. Stir in lemon juice and serve.

249 Kartoffelsuppe (German Potato Soup)

1 lb peeled-weight old potatoes,
1 oz flour,
1 oz butter,
2 rounded tablespoonsful freshly
*   milled parsley heads,*
1 large grated onion,

1 sprig fresh or 1 teaspoonful
*   dried marjoram,*
2¼ pints bone stock,
2 fat parsley stalks,
salt and pepper.

Dice potatoes, add in roomy pan to stock, onion, parsley stalks, herbs. Raise to boiling, steady off at simmer and maintain 30 minutes. Dissolve butter in small pan, add flour, stir to soft ball, add a little strained stock, beat until smooth, repeat, then turn over main pan contents, stir in, remove parsley stalks, sieve, emulsify or liquidise. Taste, correct seasoning, sprinkle top of each bowlful with parsley.

250 Soupe aux Tomates Provencale (Tomato Coulis Soup)

¼ pint tomato coulis (page 34),
1¼ pints strongly reduced bone
*   stock,*

salt and pepper,
2 preferably fresh basil leaves
*   or 1 flat dessertspoonful*
*   dried basil.*

Chop the basil as finely as possible. Place all ingredients together in pan, stir well, bring to the boil, correct seasoning and serve. For those who have a stockpot, this is a maximum 10-minute soup. In moments of great emergency and assuming you have basic tomato coulis for storing in your home, you can recourse to adding a tin of consommé diluted with tap water.

251 Minestrone

3–4 parsley stalks,
4 oz white haricot beans, overnight soaked in cold water,
4 finely chopped medium onions,
2–3 peeled crushed garlic cloves,
3 oz de-rinded streaky bacon
  or diced raw lean ham,
6–8 bacon rinds,
4 oz very thinly sliced raw tight
  white cabbage,
2 finely chopped celery hearts,
grated Parmesan cheese,
plenty of good, bone stock,

1 bouquet garni,
1 large diced raw potato,
4 medium or 6 small ripe
  tomatoes,
4 fluid oz water,
generous pinch nutmeg,
generous pinch basil,
3 oz one inch pieces vermicelli,
6 oz diced green beans,
2 medium leeks finely chopped,
salt and pepper.

Strain white beans, place in roomy pan with parsley stalks, prepared onions, garlic cloves, bacon or ham, bacon rinds, cabbage, celery hearts, potato, herbs, green beans and leeks. Cover liberally with clear bone stock. Bring to slow rolling boil. Remove scum which forms on top. Refresh with ½ a tumbler of cold water. Steady off at slow simmer, maintain 2½ hours. Meanwhile, skin and rough-cut the tomatoes. Place in a very small pan with ½ pint stock. Simmer until tender. Add basil, (fresh or dry) nutmeg, then rub through sieve, add to cooked soup in pan with vermicelli. Cook 5 minutes, correct seasoning and serve.

Note: Because you "eat" rather than "drink" this soup, with liberal sprinklings of given Parmesan cheese (handed separately) we break normal rule to suggest you use well-heated soup plates. This soup re-heats beautifully and if it over-thickens, merely add more stock and bring to boil before serving.

252 Andalusian Soup

1 large chopped onion,
1 oz butter and 1 oz oil or
  2 oz pork fat,
½ lb rough-cut potatoes,
2 tablespoonsful concentrated
  tomato purée,

1¾ pints strong stock,
1 bouquet garni,
3 tablespoonsful grated hard
  cheese,
salt and pepper.

Heat butter with oil or pork fat in roomy pan. When "singing" soft-fry onion until tender. Add all ingredients except seasonings and cheese. Simmer until all is tender. Remove herbs, sieve, emulsify or liquidise. Taste, correct seasoning, re-heat with stirred-in-cheese.

253 Kalsoppe mit Frikadeller (Norwegian Cabbage Soup with Meat Balls)

1 small, tight, white cabbage,   *2 oz dripping,*
4 pints good bone stock,   *6 peppercorns,*
1 oz butter and 1 oz oil,   *salt.*

Halve cabbage and excavate stem on both halves. Coarse grate these, then shred rest of cabbage extremely finely. Fry in hot oil/ butter or dripping until well collapsed but not browned. Turn into roomy pan, add boiling stock with peppercorns tied into muslin, simmer 2½ hours. Taste, correct seasoning, fish out pepper bag and serve (essentially) with Frikadeller (page 15).

254 Grauwe Erwertensuppe (Dutch Black Bean Soup)

10 oz dried black beans,   *paprika,*
2 quarts strong bone stock,   *salt and pepper,*
1 medium onion chopped fine,   *1 torn bay leaf,*
1 oz dripping,   *grated nutmeg,*
1 oz flour,   *8 bacon rinds.*

Soak beans overnight in cold water, strain, put in pan with stock and bay leaf, boil, skim, add bacon rinds, simmer 2 hours. Meanwhile heat dripping, fry onions gently until soft, sprinkle flour over, sprinkle with 1 heaped teaspoonful paprika powder. At end of simmering time, ladle some soup on to this paste, stir until creamy, repeat twice more, beat well and beat into soup. Simmer on 15 minutes longer, excavate rinds, strain half liquor into jug, sievc, emulsify or liquidise the rest. Return to pan, add strained liquor, bring to boil, taste, correct seasoning, add a further sprinkling of paprika to each bowlful and hand narrow strips of plain, toasted bread separately.

255 Soupe au Pistou

This Provençale Vegetable Soup is filling, family, a Southern French cousin to Italian Minestrone.

¼ pint diced runner beans,
¼ lb overnight-soaked haricot
    beans,
3 medium diced old potatoes,
2 topped tailed diced baby
    marrows (courgettes),

4 medium skinned, diced
    tomatoes,
salt and pepper,
2 oz broken (small) macaroni,
1 flat teaspoonful chopped
    fresh basil or dried crumbled,
2 oz broken (small) macaroni,
1 flat teaspoonful chopped
    fresh basil or dried crumbled,
stock.

Place all ingredients except seasonings into roomy pan and cover generously with stock. Bring to slow, rolling boil, skim and simmer until haricots are *almost* tender. Stir in macaroni previously placed in sieve with boiling water poured over. Resume simmering until macaroni is cooked but not flabby! Correct seasoning, add basil and hand fried croûtons (page 17) and grated hard cheese separately.

256 Gulasleves (Hungarian Goulasch Soup)

1 lb finely chopped onions,
2 fat, ripe tomatoes,
¾ lb lean stewing steak cut into
    matchsticks,
2 heaped tablespoonsful real
    paprika powder,
3 medium old potatoes cut into
    matchsticks,
1 red and 1 green medium
    pimento,

3 pints strong beef-bone stock,
salt and pepper,
3 oz clean beef dripping or
    dissolved raw pork fat,
1 flat tablespoonful concentrated
    tomato purée,
2 tablespoonsful wine vinegar,
½ oz flour,
1 bouquet garni.

Heat 2 oz chosen fat in frying pan. Turn meat in flour, add to "singing" fat, fry briskly until just stiffened and well coloured, remove, add remaining 1 oz fat and fry onions until golden in pan residue. Place both in roomy pan. Fry de-pipped, pithed, diced pimentoes in pan residue. Add with all other ingredients except salt and pepper and simmer steadily for 1½ hours. Then raise to hard boil and boil/stir for 3 minutes to reduce a little. Fish out herbs. Correct seasoning and serve with dumplings (page 19).

257 Nettle Soup

1¼ lb very young spring nettles,   *6 chipolatas,*
½ lb sorrel with stalks removed,   *1 carton soured cream,*
1 quart strong veal bone stock,   *1 flat teaspoonful fennel or dill.*

Pick nettle leaves off stems. Shred, and shred stemless sorrel. Add to boiling stock and poach 5 minutes. Grill chipolatas, cut into small rounds, add to soup, correct seasoning and either stir cream into soup or serve in blobs over each serving, scattering finely chopped dill or fennel lightly overall.

258 Creole Corn Soup

This is one of the most popular Creole summer soups.

1 lb rib of beef,   *1 red (hot) pepper, de-seeded,*
4 pints beef-bone stock,   *1 oz butter,*
¼ lb slightly over-ripe tomatoes,   *1 oz flour,*
3 heads corn-on-cob,   *salt and pepper.*

Pour boiling water to cover over beef rib. Leave 3 minutes. Rinse, wipe and begin. Put neatly cut rib pieces in roomy pan with stock, raise to boiling, skim carefully, "refresh" with 5 fluid oz cold water, settle at "simmer" and maintain for 1½ hours or until meat falls away from bones. Add tomatoes and conveniently-cut pieces corn cobs. Simmer on extremely gently for a further 2 hours. Remove corn pieces, scrape clean then chop corn kernels. Strain pan contents. When sufficiently cool remove flesh from bones, shred through fingers into little shreds, fish out tomato skins, return pan with corn. Taste, correct seasoning, add finely diced pepper. Simmer on for 10 minutes. Meanwhile, dissolve butter, stir in flour to form soft ball, cook 3 minutes, add ladlefuls of simmering soup, stirring between each addition. After using one third, turn on to remainder in pan. Simmer 25 minutes. Serve with toasted French bread.

259 Crème de Navettes

This **must** be made with young, small turnips and should have one or two tops added.

1 lb young turnips,	½ oz sugar,
1 or 2 well washed small turnip tops,	1½ pints white bone stock,
1 oz butter,	½ pint boiling milk,
1 oz oil,	¼ pint single cream,
salt and pepper,	1 stick of white celery.

Peel and steam turnips 5 minutes with well-washed tops. Slice turnips, chop tops and simmer both in "singing" butter and oil with pinch of salt and sugar until almost tender. Meanwhile simmer down stock to ¾ pint, with sliced turnips and celery therein. Blend contents of both pans. Sieve or emulsify. Dilute over heat with given boiling milk, correct seasoning, stir in cream and simmer 5 minutes longer. Serve with fried croûtons (page 17).

260 Soupe de la Nuit de Noce (Honeymoon Soup—for two, naturally!)

2 medium onions,	1 pint boiling water,
1 garlic clove,	salt and pepper,
1 rounded tablespoonful duck or goose fat,	1 rounded tablespoonful crushed vermicelli.
2 large skinned tomatoes,	

Chop peeled onions finely, quarter tomatoes. Fry both with garlic in hot fat until onions thoroughly yellow. Stir in water, allow to boil, steady off at simmer and maintain 30 minutes, emulsify or liquidise then sieve. Return to heat, bring to boil and stir in vermicelli. Simmer with asbestos mat between flame and pan base for further 10 minutes. Taste and correct seasoning. Meanwhile, dry out 4 slices from French "flute" in oven, low position and temperature. Place slices in base of 2 large heated bowls. Pour soup over bread and serve—in bed!

261 French Nursery Soup (Potage à l'Orge)

4 oz pearl barley,
1 large finely-chopped onion,
1 large finely-chopped leek,
1 large finely-chopped stick
   celery,
3 medium finely-chopped carrots,
1 fluid oz oil,
salt and white pepper,

9 fluid oz milk,
2 fluid oz single cream,
1 rounded dessertspoonful
   scissored chives,
20 fluid oz chicken stock
   (page 125),
1 oz butter.

Soak pearl barley 12 hours in cold, salted water. Heat oil with butter, turn in vegetables, turn and thoroughly cover and cook gently with occasional shakes for 10 minutes. Rinse pearl barley in cold water and add with chicken stock. Simmer gently for 27 minutes adding milk at 20 minutes. Correct seasonings, put in heated tureen, add cream, scatter chives on surface but do not mix.

262 Peruvian Avocado Soup

3 medium, skinned, rough-cut
   tomatoes,
1 crushed garlic clove,
1 flat teaspoonful salt,
generous pinch pepper,
1 mean, flat eggspoonful dry
   English mustard,
2 fluid oz oil,
2 oz flour,

1½ pints chicken stock A or B
   (page 125),
1 tablespoonful concentrated
   tomato purée,
3 avocados,
6 fluid oz single cream,
1 tiny pot of so-called "red
   caviare" which is really cod's
   roe!

Heat oil and fry tomatoes with garlic until both are collapsed. Stir in salt, pepper, mustard and flour and work with back of wooden spoon to a paste. Dilute gradually with stock and add tomato purée. Turn into a roomy pan and simmer for 10 minutes. Meanwhile peel, halve and stone avocados. Mash 2½ with a fork, turn into soup and simmer on. Slice remaining half avocado with silver knife and squeeze a little lemon juice over slices to stop them from blackening. After 10 minutes further simmering, emulsify pan mixture and return to pan. Stir in cream and if you wish to be true to soup's origin (we do not!) turn in cod's roe, stir until boiling and serve. Scatter slices of avocado on top.

263 Dutch Tomato Soup

1 oz butter,
½ oz flour,
2 shallots or 1 small onion,
one 2½ oz tin tomato purée,
½ pint bone stock,

½ pint water,
pepper, salt, sugar,
2 oz grated, hard Gouda cheese,
1 dessertspoonful freshly milled
*   parsley heads.*

Heat butter, fry finely chopped onion until a good yellow. Add purée and flow work in, add heated water gradually, beating between each addition, stir in hot stock, a generous pinch of sugar, correct seasoning, simmer for 10/12 minutes, i.e. until onion is tender. Pour into heated bowls, scatter with cheese and parsley.

264 Pomidorova Zupa (Ukrainian Tomato Soup)

2 very large beef marrow bones,
1 large diced carrot,
1 large diced onion,
5 oz very finely shredded
*   cabbage,*
3 pints strong beef bone stock,
2 lb over-ripe tomatoes,
1 scant flat dessertspoonful salt,
1 rounded teaspoonful castor
*   sugar,*

1 rounded coffeespoonful black
*   pepper,*
1½ oz flour,
1 carton soured cream,
4 oz cooked, risotto rice,
optional 2 rounded teaspoonsful
*   fresh finely chopped dill,*
1 rounded tablespoonful freshly
*   milled parsley heads.*

Place bones tied in muslin, carrot, onion, cabbage and stock in roomy pan, boil, skim and simmer 1 hour. Add rough-cut tomatoes, salt, sugar, pepper and re-simmer 45 minutes. Remove bones and sieve, emulsify or liquidise the rest. Mix flour and cream to smooth paste, pour on 1 teacup of soup and stir in. When smooth, turn both soup and flour paste together into pan. Stir very thoroughly. Scoop out marrow from beef bones, rough chop and return to soup, re-heat to just below boiling. Place a spoonful of rice in each heated bowl, pour soup over and scatter with dill and parsley.

265 Purée de Choux de Bruxelles

½ lb steamed Brussels sprouts,   ½ oz butter,
1 pint basic white sauce   salt and pepper,
  (page 14),   extra milk.
1 oz grated hard cheese,

Sieve sprouts or emulsify with ¼ pint white sauce. Turn into pan
with remaining white sauce, stir in cheese over moderate heat,
dilute gradually with additional milk until desired consistency is
achieved, taste, correct seasoning, stir in butter in tiny flakes.

266 Cerbah (Humble Arabic Soup)

4 large thinly-sliced onions,.   salt and pepper,
2 fluid oz oil,   2 pints strong bone stock,
4 medium rough-cut tomatoes,   strained juice 1 small lemon,
2 fat heads finely chopped mint,   12 fingers of toasted bread,
1 large red pimento,   1½ oz stale grated cheese.

Heat oil, fry onions gently until soft, work in tomatoes, then de-
pithed and pipped shredded pimento, fry on until all are soft. Turn
into roomy pan, add stock, mint and simmer gently 45 minutes.
Stir in lemon juice, correct seasoning, cover toast fingers with
cheese, float on top of soup filled heat-resistant bowls and bubble
cheese tops under moderate grill.

267 Soupe à l'Oignon Oporto

This is an extension of Soupe à l'Oignon with 1 deletion (the cheese-
toasted French bread) and two additions.

For ingredients, please turn to Soupe à l'Oignon (page 150).
After completion and before adding bread and cheese, emulsify
and return to pan. At moment of service, break four eggs into a
soup tureen. Whisk with 6 fluid oz of a modest port. Then, when
soup is again piping hot, pour on to egg mixture whisking thoroughly to ensure perfect blending. Serve immediately.

268 Soupe Polonaise

3 finely chopped hard-boiled
   eggs,
1 large crushed garlic clove,
pepper,
strained juice 1 large lemon,
12 paper-thin slices un-skinned
   cucumber,

1 egg,
1 lb sorrel,
1 or 2 lb spinach,
1 quart strongly-reduced bone
   stock.

Wash and remove sorrel and spinach stalks. Pack leaves into saucepan. Set over thread of heat. Stir and allow to collapse. After 7 minutes, sieve, stir in hard egg, garlic, lemon juice and quartered cucumber slices. Beat raw egg, strain on and beat in RAW. Pour on boiling stock (off heat remember!) stir very thoroughly, taste, season, refrigerate when cooled. When icy serve with ice cubes in each bowl.

269 Soupe Savoyarde

white and green of 2 trimmed
   leeks,
1 large or 2 medium chopped
   turnips,
6 oz chopped onions,
3 oz dripping or dissolved pork
   fat,

2 very large old potatoes
   coarse-grated,
1½ pints milk,
2 crustless slices from
   sandwich loaf,
4 oz any melting cheese,
2½ pints stock or water,
salt and pepper.

Slice leeks thinly. Heat chosen fat until "singing", soft-fry leeks and onions slowly, when collapsed add remaining vegetables, fry on stir/turning 5 minutes. Scrape into roomy lidded casserole, add stock and milk. Cover and oven/cook 310 F (gas 2) mid-shelf 2 hours. Serve from pot, napkin-wrapped. Cut bread into 8 triangles. Deep fry till brown. Float on top. Grate cheese and pile on top.

Les Crèmes

270. Cream of Cheddar Soup
271. Crème de Cresson
272. Crème de Chou-Fleur d'Italie
273. Crème d'Epinards
274. Crème des Oeufs
275. Cream of Broccoli Soup
276. Crème au Mais Simple
277. Crème Americaine
278. Sengalese Cream Soup
279. Geflugelrahm Suppe
280. Crème de Crevettes
281. Crème Soubise Tomatée
282. Crème Forestière
283. Consommé à la Crème (Fritter Batter)
284. Tourin de Perigord
285. Crème Chanoinesse
286. Peanut Cream Soup
287. Crème Carmelite
288. Crème de Crosnes
289. Crème aux Pointes d'Asperges
290. Soupe Béchamel
291. Almond Soup
292. Crème Judic
293. Crème Parmentier
294. Crème St-Germain
295. Germiny
296. Crème Aurore
297. Cream of Chicory Soup
298. Tarragon Cream Soup
299. Cream of Jerusalem Artichoke Soup (English)
300. Crème Dubarry
301. Crème de Concombres Glacé
302. Chicken and Almond Soup
303. Mustard Soup
304. Egg Soup

270 Cream of Cheddar Soup

1 pint hot milk,
1 oz butter,
1 crushed garlic clove,
½ lb very thinly diced Cheddar,
¼ pint cold milk,
1 oz flour,

3 generous pinches nutmeg,
3 generous pinches pepper,
5 fluid oz dry white cooking
  wine,
2 egg yolks,
4 fluid oz single cream.

Put garlic and butter into hot milk and stir over very low heat 3 minutes. Put moist Cheddar into liquidiser or emulsifier with cold milk, flour, nutmeg and pepper. Switch on and maintain fast until creamy. Turn into top of double saucepan over hot water with garlic milk. Stir well, stir in wine, blend egg yolks with cream, stir in a little soup, return to bulk in top pan. Stir carefully from bottom until piping hot but DO NOT BOIL. Season with salt, pepper and nutmeg. Hand diced fried croûtons (page 17) separately.

271 Crème de Cresson (Watercress and Potato Soup)

2 bunches watercress,
1½ lb potatoes,
½ pint stock and 1½ pints milk,

salt and pepper to season,
1 oz butter.

Rough-cut potatoes, steam and then sieve. Pick off stems from watercress, place stems in chosen fluid, bring to boil, simmer gently until tender. Strain, Stir sieved, cooked potatoes into liquor, chop cooked watercress leaves finely, stir into soup. Season to taste, stir in butter and serve.

272 Crème de Chou-Fleur d'Italie

This is Velouté de Chou-Fleur d'Italie (page 62) enhanced as follows:

given soup (page 62),
2 separated egg yolks,

5 fluid oz single cream.

Blend yolks with cream. Ensure soup is piping hot. Place asbestos mat over flame or turn into double pan over hot water. Pour a little of Velouté on to egg/cream, stir, return to pan, stir again **very carefully** until once again **hot** but not boiling. Service with Cheese Straws (page 22).

273 Crème d'Epinards

(Spinach should always be cooked as given below.)

1 lb green, washed spinach with
   coarse stems removed,
½ oz butter
¼ level eggspoonful nutmeg,
½ level eggspoonful cinnamon,

¾ pint milk,
salt and pepper,
¼ pint single cream or top-of-
   the-milk.

Place spinach in thick pan and set over very low heat. Stir until collapsed (maximum 7 minutes). Sieve, emulsify or liquidise, add all remaining ingredients, with seasonings to taste, simmer 10 minutes. Serve.

274 Crème des Oeufs

1 pint milk,
1 pint chicken stock A or B
   (page 125),
3 standard eggs,
6 fluid oz single cream,

1 oz butter,
1 oz flour,
salt and pepper,
1 flat teaspoonful paprika
   powder.

Soften butter, work in flour and paprika to form a soft ball. Dilute gradually with stock, beating well between each addition. Stir in milk. Allow to simmer gently while whipping eggs and stirring single cream into them. After 10 minutes simmering, turn soup into top of double saucepan over boiling water and low flame. Pour a little soup over egg/cream mixture, stir very thoroughly, turn on to soup and continue stirring. Taste, correct seasoning. Hard grated hard cheese separately.

275 Cream of Broccoli Soup

$\frac{1}{2}$ pint sauce Soubise (page 17),
2 pints milk,
4 steamed heads purple-
sprouting broccoli,

$\frac{1}{4}$ pint double cream,
1 large or 2 small eggs,
salt and pepper,
1 oz butter.

Emulsify cooked broccoli with $\frac{1}{4}$ pint milk, fold resultant purée into remaining boiling milk, add cream and simmer 5 minutes. Blend beaten eggs with a little cream mixture, pour on a little hot soup, stir, turn remainder into top of double pan over boiling water, add Soubise. Turn egg mix into pan contents, stir carefully until smooth and creamy. Correct seasoning, stir in butter in small flakes. Optionally hand grated hard cheese separately.

276 Crème au Maïs Simple

14 oz tin sweet corn containing
chopped pimento,
$\frac{3}{4}$ pint chicken stock (A or B
page 125),

$\frac{1}{4}$ pint top-of-milk or single
cream,
salt and pepper.

Mix all given ingredients with salt and pepper to taste. Heat through, serve plain or sieve, emulsify or liquidise. Hand Pulled Bread (page 12) separately.

277 Crème Americaine (Escoffier approved!)

3 pints chicken stock (A or B
page 125),
1 standard tin concentrated
tomato soup,
4 oz tapioca,

pinch salt,
$\frac{1}{2}$ oz butter,
1 dessertspoonful potted
shrimp paste,
pepper.

Blend stock, tinned soup, tapioca and salt in roomy pan. Simmer 15 minutes. Stir in butter, shrimp paste, pepper to taste. Simmer further 10 minutes. Serve with Diablotins (page 12).

278 Sengalese Cream Soup (Hot and heavy on cream!)

2 medium chopped onions,
2 outside celery stalks chopped,
2 small cooking apples, peeled,
 then chopped,
2 fluid oz oil,
1 dessertspoonful Masala paste,
1 oz flour,
1¾ pints chicken stock (A or B
 page 125),

salt and pepper,
generous pinch chilli powder,
generous pinch cayenne,
½ pint whipping or double
 cream,
4 oz diced, cooked chicken
 meat.

Heat oil in frying pan, soft-fry onions 5 minutes, then celery and apple 3 minutes. Work in Masala and flour to thick paste, dilute gradually with stock, stirring until smooth after each addition. When pan is full emulsify, liquidise or sieve. Turn into roomy pan. Add remaining stock, chilli and cayenne. Taste, correct seasoning, stir in boiled cream and chicken flesh.

279 Geflugelrahm Suppe (Austrian Cream of Chicken Soup)

1 small boiling fowl,
4 peeled, quartered, good-sized
 onions,
1 large chopped carrot,
white of 1 fat leek sliced finely,
1 large celery stalk (with leaves)
 chopped small,

1 scraped parsley root or
 3 stems,
salt and pepper,
2 egg yolks,
6 fluid oz double cream,
6 pints chicken stock (A or B
 page 125).

Smash up fowl with mallet or metal meat batter until bones are cracked and broken. Place in lidded casserole with onions and stock. Cover and cook 335 F (gas 3) centre shelf 3 hours or 240 F (gas ¼) lowest shelf overnight, say 11 p.m.–8 a.m. Strain thoroughly. Place liquor in roomy pan. Simmer down to 4 pints. Add prepared vegetables and parsley. Simmer on 35 minutes. Strain into clean pan, draw to extreme edge of heat. Beat egg yolks with cream, when soup is just below boiling, pour on a little, stir thoroughly, correct seasoning, turn into bulk in pan stir very carefully and if re-heating turn into top of double pan over hot water to avoid curdling.

280 Crème de Crevettes

(Delicious whether made with little brown or pink shrimps.)

2 pints water,
1 large "leaf" lemon peel,
½ pint shelled shrimps, plus
    shrimp shells and heads,
1 lb white fish trimmings,
2 parsley stalks,

1 small sprig fennel,
¼ pint dry white cooking wine,
¼ pint single cream,
1½ oz butter,
1¼ oz flour,
pepper.

Place all shells, heads, fish trimmings, lemon, parsley and fennel in roomy pan, cover with given water, raise to boiling point, simmer fairly strongly 20 minutes. Strain thoroughly, discard shells etc. Dissolve butter in pan, stir in flour to soft ball, dilute gradually with small additions wine, beating well between each addition. Repeat with strained fish stock (previously simmered down to 1 pint). When all is absorbed and soup smooth, add all but 1 tablespoonful chopped shrimps and cream, then taste, correct pepper seasoning, float one or two reserve shrimps over each serving.

281 Crème Soubise Tomatée

1 pint Soubise (page 17),
¼ pint single cream,
6 very ripe tomatoes,
6 fluid oz white stock,

salt and pepper,
1 oz grated hard cheese ideally
    Parmesan,
1 fat parsley stalk.

Rough-cut tomatoes, add stock and parsley stalk, simmer while stirring until juices flow. Then simmer on until tomatoes are collapsed. Remove parsley stalk, sieve or emulsify on to Soubise. Heat through gently, thinning with additional stock as desired. Correct flavour with seasonings. Stir in cream, put a little cheese in bottom of each heated soup-bowl. Add soup and serve. If preferred, this soup may be further flavoured with a teaspoonful of powdered paprika stirred into Soubise before blending with next ingredient.

282 Crème Forestière

½ lb onions,
1 lb mushrooms,
2 pints chicken, veal or pork
   stock,
½ pint dry white wine,

1 oz butter,
1 oz flour,
salt and pepper,
1 oz olive oil,
½ pint cream.

Peel onions and slice very thinly, then chop small. Dissolve and heat butter and oil in large thick frying pan. Add onions and fry with asbestos mat between flame and pan to ensure onions collapse without browning. When uniformly soft and yellow, add very thinly sliced, chopped *un*-skinned mushrooms and their stalks. Work in until collapsed and juices are running freely. Scatter flour over and work down to a paste with the back of a wooden spoon. Add wine gradually, working up between each addition to smooth consistency. Scrape frying pan contents into a saucepan, stir in all stock slowly. Bring to the boil and then simmer for 20 minutes. Taste, correct seasonings, stir in cream, re-raise to boiling point and serve.

283 Consommé à la Crème

2 pints clear chicken or veal
   consommé,
½ pint single cream,
4 separated egg yolks,

8 slices thin, crustless buttered
   bread,
1 small glass jar inexpensive
   Danish caviare,
fritter batter.

Heat and season the clear strained consommé. Blend the egg yolks and the cream together. At table present a tureen containing the eggs and the cream. Whisk in the consommé gradually and serve with the buttered bread slices de-crusted and caviare spread, cut into triangular sandwiches, then dipped in the fritter batter and deep-fried to a rich golden brown.

Fritter Batter

2 heaped tablespoonsful sifted
  flour,
1 generous pinch salt,

1 standard egg,
1 scant tablespoonful olive oil,
cold water.

Place flour in small bowl, make well in centre, put in oil and salt, add beaten egg and blend thoroughly with scant water additions to thick coating consistency. Rest batter 2 hours before using, please.

---

284 Tourin de Perigord

6 oz finely chopped peeled
  onions,
1 oz butter or chicken or pork
  fat,
1 extra oz butter,
1 rounded tablespoonful flour,
34 fluid oz milk,

2 separated egg yolks,
$\frac{1}{4}$ pint single cream,
6 rounds French (flute) bread
  cut $\frac{1}{2}$ inch thick or Pulled
  Bread (page 12),
salt and pepper.

Soften onions in hot chosen fat until thoroughly yellow. Dust flour over, work down to rough paste with back of wooden spoon. Add boiling milk gradually, beating well between each addition, until thin sauce is obtained then stir in remainder and simmer with extreme gentleness 25 minutes. Mix cream and eggs together smoothly. Stir into cooked soup, off heat, until thickened. Do not allow to boil again. Taste, correct seasoning and either pour immediately into soup bowls or re-heat in top of double saucepan over hot water. Either way, stir remaining ounce of butter in at last. Slide 1 or 2 slices of toast over surface and serve immediately.

---

285 Crème Chanoinesse

Follow recipe for Crème Carmelite (page 173), substituting, for sole matchsticks, 4 oz soft herring roes. Cook as explained, dice

172

roes small, set aside and cook a further 2 oz of herring roes as before, sieve, stir into fish stock and proceed as instructed in that recipe.

286 Peanut Cream Soup

(Many people detest peanut butter; there are those who like it immensely!)

2 pints milk,
¾ pint very well-reduced pork or bacon bone stock (if using bacon add salt carefully),

6 oz peanut butter,
1 oz potato flour or arrowroot,
5 fluid oz single cream,
salt and pepper.

Heat milk and stock together. Put peanut butter into roomy bowl, thin down very gradually with hot liquors, return to pan, stir in chosen thickening blended with single cream, and stir on over moderate heat for 5 minutes. Correct seasoning.

287 Crème Carmelite

2 pints fish stock (page 106),
1½ oz chicken or pork fat or butter,
1½ oz flour,
6 oz single cream,

2 eggs,
1 sole fillet (4 oz),
4 fluid oz dry white cooking wine,
salt and pepper.

Cut sole into matchsticks, place in a tiny pan with a flake of given butter and the wine. Simmer extremely gently 3–4 minutes. Strain, set aside sole add liquor to fish stock. Dissolve butter over moderate heat. Work in flour to soft ball, dilute gradually with stock, beating well between each addition. Stir in cream, simmer 5 minutes, slide in sole matchsticks, stir again, taste, correct seasoning and optionally sprinkle milled parsley over servings.

288 Crème de Crosnes

This delicate Japanese vegetable produces an equally delicate soup which will intrigue people. These vegetables are very easy to grow.

1 lb Japanese Artichokes,
1 pint boiling milk,
2 medium-sized, sliced potatoes,
1 sprig chervil when available,

2 oz butter,
salt and pepper,
cut lemon.

Skin artichokes after steaming 7 minutes, then slice. Heat 1 oz butter in a saucepan and turn slices in this for 4 minutes. Add milk, chervil and potatoes. Simmer very gently until completely tender. Emulsify or sieve, add a squeeze or two of lemon juice, correct seasoning, run softened butter through fingers into soup then stir in cream.

289 Crème aux Pointes d'Asperges

Pray do not be fooled by big fat asparagus. The very best flavour is in sprew—the name given to the thin, spindly shoots which often precede the appearance of those fat asparagus stems. Use sprew for soups.

1 lb sprew,
1½ pints chicken stock A or B
  (page 125),
¼ pint single cream or top-of-
  milk,

salt and pepper,
1 oz butter,
1 oz flour,
¼ pint dry, white-cooking-type
  wine.

Begin by washing and steaming sprew. When tender, chop off tiny heads, set aside. Put remainder into emulsifier with 5 fluid oz chicken stock. When emulsified, rub through sieve to separate the stringy strands from purée. Then soften butter in thick pan, stir in flour to roux gradually with wine, beating well between additions.

Repeat with chicken stock, then stir in purée and finally cream. When all is bubbling merrily, taste, correct seasoning and serve in bowls. Float reserved asparagus heads on top with a light, optional sprinkling of parsley.

290 Soupe Béchamel

This is nothing more than soup Velouté (page 19) with 1 separated egg yolk blended thoroughly with 4 fluid oz double cream, so *beware* of making Velouté too thick. If it looks like being so, after extra thickening agents have been added, dilute with extra milk *before* adding the egg/cream mix which is then scraped back into the bulk of Velouté and then immediately turned into the top of a double saucepan over hot water to avoid any risk of curdling. Stir and serve.

291 Almond Soup (Norman in origin, adapted)

2 oz sweet almonds, milled
  finely,
1½ pints milk,
½ pint single cream,
1 oz flour,
1 oz butter,

1 small head celery,
1 shallot or small onion,
salt, pepper and 1 level
  teaspoonful fine sugar,
2 separated egg yolks.

Place hot milk, whole onion, celery head and milled almonds in top of double saucepan over hot water and poach for 1½ hours. Remove celery head and onion and sieve or emulsify. Dissolve fat in small pan, add flour, stir to soft ball, add liquor gradually, stirring carefully between each addition. Add cream stirring all the time. Season lightly with salt, pepper and sugar. Stir in purée, blend yolks and cream. Pour a little hot soup over mixture. Stir thoroughly. Turn remainder into top of double saucepan over hot water. Remove from heat, stir egg mix into soup. Re-set over base pan and stir carefully until creamy and thickened.

292 Crème Judic

1 large, well-washed, wiped,
* shredded Cos lettuce,*
¾ pint Béchamel (page 14),
½ pint well-reduced, flavoursome
* white bone stock,*
* salt and pepper,*

6 bacon rinds,
1 oz butter,
2 oz finely chopped or minced
* white of chicken or ham or*
* gammon.*

Sizzle bacon rinds until crisp in small frying pan. Remove, add lettuce and fry gently until collapsed. Add to Béchamel in saucepan, dilute with stirred-in stock; simmer 8 minutes, taste, correct seasoning and pour into bowls. Blend butter with chosen dice, reserving some so that you can drop small blobs on top of each serving.

293 Crème Parmentier

Please turn to Purée Parmentièr (page 48). The Crème is merely an extension of this recipe. Follow the purée directions through to after emulsifying or sieving stage. Then dilute over low heat with gradual addition of single cream. Finally stir in 1 oz butter in tiny flakes and hand little squares of brown bread spread with Chervil Butter (page 16).

294 Crème St-Germain

Please turn to Purée St-Germain (page 52). Follow recipe through to addition of stock. Add only ½ pint stock, then 7 fluid oz of best milk and finally 7 fluid oz single cream. Season, omit butter flakes and when in (heated) bowls, use 2 fluid oz whipped, double cream for folding in with extra peas, reserving some to drop in blobs or use for piped rosettes over centre top of each serving.

295 Germiny

1 lb well-washed, carefully
   picked sorrel,
4 oz butter,
1 pint white stock

4 separated egg yolks,
salt and pepper,
¼ pint thick cream.

Place 3 oz butter in thick pan over medium heat, dissolve, add sorrel and reduce to pulp in maximum of 8 minutes. Sieve, add stock and correct seasoning. Pour into top of double saucepan over hot water. At moment of service, beat eggs and cream together, pour on to heated soup and whisk until hot *but not boiling*. Stir in final ounce of butter in tiny flakes.

You may be surprised to know that this soup, made thin and chilled until icy cold is quite wonderful in hot weather.

296 Crème Aurore

1 pint Velouté (page 19),
1 generous tablespoonful
   concentrated tomato purée,

¼ pint single cream,
1 oz softened butter,
salt and pepper.

Blend purée into Velouté over moderate heat; stir in cream, season to taste and finish by rubbing butter in flakes through fingers. Stir well and serve.

297 Cream of Chicory Soup

3 medium heads chicory,
1 pint boiling water,

4 lumps sugar.

Place chicory in a pan, pour over boiling water, add sugar and cook for 3 minutes over low heat. Drain, wipe and use exactly as given for Crème Dubarry (page 178), substituting prepared chicory for cauliflower.

298 Tarragon Cream Soup

6 small tarragon heads (2 inches
    long, finely chopped),
1 tablespoonful each of milled
    parsley and chervil,
2 tiny, finely chopped shallots,
2 oz softened butter,

1 level teaspoonful French
    mustard,
2 lightly forked egg-yolks,
½ pint milk,
½ pint single cream,
salt and pepper.

Blend tarragon and shallots with other herbs. Put butter, mustard, egg yolks and herbs into top of double pan over boiling water and low heat. Stir over heat while pouring in cream slowly. Do not stop stirring. As mixture thickens, be careful to scrape from base edges, add milk gradually until all is absorbed. Taste, correct seasoning and serve immediately.

299 Cream of Jerusalem Artichoke Soup (English)

2 lb Jerusalem artichokes,
    steamed, then skinned
    thereafter,
1 oz butter,
1 pint white stock,
1 pint milk,

1 blade mace,
1 outer stick celery,
2 tablespoonsful thick cream,
cayenne and salt,
1 oz flour.

Sieve or emulsify cooked artichokes. Boil milk with mace, chopped celery and 1 fat pinch cayenne. Strain. Dissolve butter in thick pan, stir in flour. When formed into soft ball add stock, gradually beating until smooth after each addition. Then stir in artichoke purée, then milk and bring to the boil. Simmer over low heat *and asbestos mat* for 20 minutes. Taste, correct seasoning, stir in cream and serve.

300 Crème Dubarry

1 small trimmed cauliflower,
1 oz flour,
1 oz dripping,
salt and pepper,
stripped sprig of winter savory
    OR 1 small teaspoonful dried
    savory,

1 pint stock,
2 egg yolks,
¼ pint milk OR single cream,
1 oz grated hard cheese.

Pare green from cauliflower leaves, remove core of central stem, break up flower, add with green to stock and simmer until tender. Emulsify or sieve. Dissolve fat in small pan, stir in flour, stir to soft ball, cook on while stirring for 3 minutes. Thin gradually with milk, then whip in purée. Taste and correct seasoning. Add savory. Finally bring back to boiling point, stir in cheese until completely dissolved. Remove from heat. Beat up egg yolks, pour on a little soup, stir/scrape back into pan and stir again very thoroughly. Serve immediately. If desiring to re-heat later, turn into top of double pan over hot water to avoid any risk of curdling.

301 Crème de Concombres Glacé

This soup depends for its quality upon the stock employed. With dissolved meat-cubes in hot water it will be just that.

1 large or 2 small cucumbers,	*¼ pint single cream,*
1 pint strong, well-flavoured	*salt and pepper,*
chicken, veal, lamb or pork	*ice cubes,*
stock,	*small separate bowlful of finely*
¼ pint milk,	*scissored, fresh chives.*

Wash, wipe and slice cucumbers paper-thin *with their skins on*. Just remove any blemished patches. Place in pan with stock, bring to boiling point, level off at steady simmer and maintain until stock has reduced to a mean ¾ pint. Emulsify or sieve. Stir into the resultant purée both the milk and cream, taste and correct seasoning. If deemed too thick for personal taste, dilute with extra milk or single cream. Just before service, since this mixture tends to thicken up during refrigeration-storage time, add an ice cube to each serving and hand chives separately.

Note: This soup may have its chives throughout the year if you lay in a freezer stock. Scissor freshly-gathered chives in season. Pack into ice-cube freezing trays and top up with cold water. Freeze, unmould, pack into polythene freezer-bags, fasten with plastic-covered closures and freeze until the night before service. Tip cubes into sieve over small bowl. Water will drain away leaving chives to be patted in a clean cloth and served as fresh. Remember too, that the same may be done with any of the half-hardy herbs.

302 Chicken and Almond Cream

2 pints chicken stock (B page 125),
1 rounded dessertspoonful freshly milled parsley heads,
5 fluid oz thick cream,
1 eggspoonful paprika powder,

8 oz chopped celery heart,
1 egg,
½ pint milk,
salt and pepper,
4 oz ground almonds,
1 oz flour.

Simmer stock, celery and ground almonds for 20 minutes giving occasional stirs. Sieve, emulsify or liquidise. Whip in bowl the egg, flour and cold milk. Pour on a little hot stock mix, stir well, turn into double pan over hot water, stir until piping hot, stir in cream, taste, correct seasoning, pour into heated bowls, sprinkle mixed paprika and parsley overall.

303 Mustard Soup

2 fluid oz thick cream,
2 oz butter,
3 flat tablespoonsful English mustard,
2 tablespoonsful cold water,
1½ oz flour,

1 pint chicken stock (A or B page 125).
½ pint best possible milk,
2 shallots or one small to medium onion,
2 separated egg yolks,
salt and white pepper.

Dissolve butter in thick pan. Stir in flour and work to soft ball. Add heated stock gradually beating thoroughly between each addition. Grate onion or shallots coarsely. Press pulp through small sieve onto soup, add milk and simmer 15 minutes. Work egg yolks with thick cream and make up mustard with water, blend both together. Pour on a little hot soup, return all to pan, stir carefully until very hot but *do not* boil. Taste, correct seasoning and serve.

304 Egg Soup

2 eggs,
1 rounded tablespoonful
   concentrated tomato purée,
2 oz grated stale cheese,
1 chopped hard boiled egg,
2 oz crumbled vermicelli,

salt and pepper,
celery salt,
2 pints boiling milk,
2 fluid oz single cream or
   top-of-milk.

Mix vermicelli into milk, simmer 5 minutes, stir in cheese, simmer until clear, turn into double pan over hot water, blend eggs with cream and purée. Pour on a little of pan mix, stir well, stir into bulk mix and continue stirring until hot and thickened. Taste, correct seasonings, pour into heated soup bowls, scatter a little chopped egg over centre of each.

Fruit Soups

305. Coconut Soup
306. Cranberry Bortsch
307. Pumpkin Soup
308. Sopa di Lima
309. Hindustani Coconut Soup
310. German Grape Harvest Soup
311. Sweet-Sour Apple and Onion Soup
312. Red Cherry Soup
313. Curry-Apple Soup
314. Iced Fruit Soup
315. German Cherry Soup
316. Soupa Augholemono

305 Coconut Soup

3 pints chicken stock (A or B
   page 125),
4 oz grated fresh coconut or
   3 oz desiccated coconut,
1 blade mace,

salt and pepper,
1 oz butter,
scant 1 oz flour,
2 fluid oz thick cream.

Place chosen coconut in pan, cover with stock. If desiccated coconut, leave steeping 1 hour first, in stock, then boil, add mace, simmer 45 minutes. Dissolve butter in small pan, work in flour, stir to soft ball, add liquor very gradually to achieve thin sauce, beat well between each addition. Return to main bulk liquor, simmer 5 minutes, correct seasoning, stir in cream and serve.

306 Cranberry Bortsch

1 lb cranberries,
3 pints cold water,
½ lb very thinly sliced tight
   white cabbage,
1 lb cooked beetroot cut into
   matchsticks,

1 medium finely chopped onion,
salt and pepper,
1 flat teaspoonful sugar,
optional soured cream,
1 rounded teaspoonful freshly
   milled parsley.

Place cranberries and water in roomy pan, bring to boil, simmer until collapsed. Sieve, add onion and cabbage, simmer until tender, stir in beetroot, correct seasoning, add sugar and serve with optional blob soured cream in centre of each serving. Sprinkle parsley lightly overall.

307 Pumpkin Soup

2¼ lb pumpkin flesh,
2 large chopped onions,
4 ripe tomatoes,
1 pint strongly-reduced chicken
   stock (A or B page 125),

salt and pepper,
3 oz cooked Patna rice,
¼ pint whipping or double cream,
1 rounded tablespoonful freshly-
   milled parsley,
2¼ pints milk.

Steam rough-cut pumpkin flesh. Simmer onions in as little stock as possible. Emulsify with pumpkin flesh, skinned de-pipped tomato flesh. Stir into remaining hot stock and milk, mixed, in roomy pan. Stir in rice. Taste and correct seasoning.

Note: Super service is in scollop-edged, hollowed out pumpkin with top sliced away first. Whipped chosen cream is dropped in large blob centrally and parsley sprinkled overall.

308 Sopa di Lima (Lime Soup—can be made with lemon)

1 medium chopped onion,
2 tablespoonsful olive oil,
3 medium tomatoes, skinned,
   cored, de-pipped,
3 pints chicken stock (A or B
   page 125),
1 flat teaspoonful oregano or
   thyme,

1 large lime (or lemon) plus
   extra skin,
2 chicken livers,
2 chicken gizzards,
2 oz diced chicken flesh,
salt and pepper.

Heat oil in frying pan, fry onions gently until soft, add tomato flesh and fry on 3 minutes. Place stock, herb, strained juice of lime or lemon with 2 lemon skins into roomy pan. Simmer 5 minutes. Remove citrus peel, add livers and gizzards, simmer 10 minutes. Stir in fried mixture, simmer gently until onion is tender. Remove gizzards and liver, discard former, chop latter finely, return to soup with chopped chicken meat. Taste, correct seasoning and serve with Tortillas.

309 Hindustani Coconut Soup

1 small coconut,
¼ flat teaspoonful mace,
salt and pepper,
2½ pints strong white bone stock,
2 separated egg yolks,

4 tablespoonsful strained lemon
juice,
1 oz flour,
¼ flat teaspoonful cinnamon
powder.

Punch holes in coconut. Drain off milk, open and cut out coconut flesh. Grate flesh, add to stock with spices, boil then simmer 30 minutes. Strain, add coconut milk, simmer on. Mix yolks with flour and lemon juice, pour on a little hot stock, stir carefully, mix into soup, stir constantly until slightly thickened, smooth and just below boiling point. Taste, correct seasoning and hand a small bowl of hot rice separately.

Note: To open coconut easily, tie string round centre and twist with metal skewer like tourniquet until very tight. Tap string all round with a small hammer and 2 halves will fall apart.

310 German Grape Harvest Soup

1 lb wine grapes red or white,
1 quart water,
1 egg yolk,

2 tablespoonsful tapioca,
salt,
castor sugar.

Peel and de-pip grapes. Emulsify in their own juice. Place in a pan with 2 fluid oz given water and 1 oz castor sugar. Simmer down slowly to syrupy pap. Add remaining water, when bubbling stir in tapioca, stir a little soup into egg yolks, stir well, pour into main soup and stir carefully till hot *but not boiling*. Optionally scatter each serving with a few peeled stoned, extra grapes, add extra sugar if desired.

311 Sweet-Sour Apple and Onion Soup

2 large peeled cooking apples
  with all flesh removed and
  chopped small,
2 large onions peeled and
  chopped small,
1½ pints milk,
1 oz flour,

3 rashers de-rinded, diced,
  streaky bacon,
1 flat eggspoonful dried oregano,
salt and pepper,
2 pinches powdered ginger,
Oignons Royale (page 16),
1 oz dripping.

Draw diced bacon in dry pan over low heat for 2 minutes. Add dripping and onions and fry gently under lid until soft but not browned. Add apples, stir and fry 4 minutes. Work in flour to form paste, then add herbs, ginger and light seasonings of salt and pepper. Dilute with a little heated milk. Stir again, scrape into a saucepan, add remaining milk and oregano and simmer gently for 12 minutes. Pour into serving bowls. Sprinkle tops with Oignons Royale.

312 Red Cherry Soup

1 lb red cherries,
4 oz Morello cherries,
4 pints cold water,
1 rounded tablespoonful potato
  flour or arrowroot,
3 extra fluid oz cold water,

thin peel and strained juice of
  1 medium lemon,
4 fluid oz cooking type "plonk"
  claret,
2 oz castor sugar.

Wash, stem and stone cherries, then simmer in bulk water with lemon peel until really tender. Remove peel, sieve, emulsify or liquidise, return to pan. Dissolve chosen thickening in extra water and stir in. When thickened, add wine, lemon juice and sugar. Serve icily chilled with optional top-sprinklings of powdered cinnamon.

313 Curry-Apple Soup

3 medium sized eating-apples
  (James Grieve are best for
  this soup),
1½ pints cleared, well-reduced
  lamb or chicken stock,

salt and pepper to season,
1 rounded teaspoonful of
  Masala paste (or curry
  powder if you must),
3 oz desiccated coconut.

Peel, then coarse-grate apples and drop into prepared stock. Bring to the boil, level off to a very gentle simmer and so poach apples until just tender. Slake the curry paste (or powder) with a spoonful or two of the fluid, stir in and simmer on for 5 minutes. Meanwhile scatter the desiccated coconut over a piece of greaseproof laid over an ordinary baking sheet. Place on topmost shelf of oven at 275 F (gas 1) and allow to become brown and crisp. Hand separately and let each person scatter a spoonful over the soup in heated bowls.

314 Iced Fruit Soup

¼ lb picked redcurrants,
¼ lb stoned white cherries,
¼ lb minced apple flesh,
¼ lb skinless orange segments,
2 oz soft brown ("pieces") or
  castor sugar,

2 lightly rounded tablespoonsful
  potato flour or arrowroot,
3 fluid oz cold water,
½ oz butter,
2¼ pints extra water,
strained juice 1 small lemon.

Simmer fruits in 2¼ pints water until tender. Emulsify, then sieve. Return to pan, add sugar, when dissolved stir mixed chosen thickening with 3 fluid oz cold water. Turn on to pan liquor, stir until soup thickens without lumping, as it will! Stir in lemon juice and butter; when completely blended, cool down, pour into glasses. Chill thoroughly, optionally sprinkle a minute quantity of finely-chopped fresh mint over each serving.

315 German Cherry Soup

½ lb Napoleon cherries,
2 oz Morello cherries,
¼ lb picked redcurrants,
½ lb raspberries,
thinly peeled rind of 1 medium
   lemon,
¼ lb castor sugar,

6 cloves,
6 fluid oz "plonk" type claret,
1 rounded tablespoonful potato
   flour or arrowroot,
3 fluid oz cold water,
1 inch stick cinnamon,
3 pints extra water.

Put all fruits and cinnamon stick and bulk water into roomy pan. Simmer until tender. Press back into pan with back of wooden spoon through ordinary sieve, but do not rub! Add lemon peel and cloves and set to simmer. Blend chosen thickening with 3 fluid oz water, turn over soup, stir until thick and smooth, then stir in claret. Serve icily chilled in glass containers.

316 Soupa Augholemono (German Lemon Soup)

2 pints chicken stock (A or B
   page 125),
2 oz rice,
2 separated egg yolks,

strained juice and lightly grated
   rind 1½ medium lemons,
1 bouquet garni,
1 leaf lemon peel and same of
   dried orange.

This soup ranges in quality from practically pond-water (when made with a chicken stock cube) to a delicate and delicious soup when made with well seasoned good quality chicken stock A or B. For everyday occasions use liquor obtained by simmering the carcase of a chicken in ordinary white meat stock until tender. For a peak of perfection, smash down an old small fowl to a sad pulp— cover liberally with cold water, add herbs, lemon and orange peels and simmer under lid or foil until poor old hen is purged of flavour. Strain, measure liquor, reduce by simmering to 2–2¼ pints, add rice, simmer again for 10 minutes, remove from heat. Beat in egg yolks, add grated lemon rind and juice, re-heat in double pan to ensure eggs do not curdle.

Beer and Wine Soups

317. Weinsuppe mit Schneeklosschen
318. Iced Beer Soup
319. The Devil's Brew
320. Yablouchni
321. Soup au vin Lyonnais
322. Perlana Weinsuppe
323. Mosellesuppe
324. Biersuppe

317 Weinsuppe mit Schneeklosschen (German Wine Soup with Whipped Egg Whites!)

1 pint Moselle wine,	*the thinly peeled rind 1 large*
½ pint boiling water,	*lemon,*
2 eggs,	*one 2 inch stick of cinnamon,*
4 flat tablespoonsful castor	*powdered cinnamon,*
sugar,	*1 oz butter,*
	1 oz flour.

Melt and heat butter in a pan. Stir in flour to soft ball stage, add boiling water gradually, beating well between each addition. Do this carefully and thoroughly or soup will be ruined! Now add wine, cinnamon stick and half given sugar. Stir over such a low heat for 10 minutes that mixture cooks but does not even simmer. Remove cinnamon and peel. Stir separated egg yolks in 1 tablespoonful soup, stir into soup again very carefully. Whip egg whites very stiffly, fold in remaining sugar, spread over soup, draw to side of stove. Rest 20 minutes. Heat gently without boiling. Ladle into heated bowls, sprinkle powdered cinnamon overall.

318 Iced Beer Soup (no cooking)

1¼ pints light beer,	*generous pinch powdered*
2 rounded teaspoonsful castor	*cinnamon,*
sugar,	*1 stiffly whipped egg white,*
1 tablespoonful strained lemon	*ice cubes,*
juice,	*4 oz crumbled pumpernickel.*
1½ cups chicken stock (A page	
125),	

Place all ingredients in a shaker and shake vigorously with crushed ice cubes in its separate container. Pour into glass bowls and serve.

319 The Devil's Brew

4 oz finely chopped shallots,	*strained juice of ½ small lemon,*
6 fluid oz ale,	*2 oz course-grated red of carrot,*
4 pints beef bone stock,	*2 oz rice,*
pinch cayenne pepper,	*1 flat dessertspoonful*
salt,	*concentrated tomato purée.*
1 eggspoonful Masala paste,	

Set stock simmering with shallots and carrots, maintain 30 minutes. Add rice, simmer 12 minutes, strain and set aside vegetables and rice. Add Masala and work in with cayenne, purée and ale. Return vegetables to liquor. Season to taste with salt, stir in lemon juice and serve.

---

320 Yablouchni (Polish in origin—"borrowed" by Russia)

6 large cored cooking apples,
1 bottle "plonk"-type claret,
strained juice and grated rind
  1 good-sized lemon,
1 tablespoonful blackcurrant
  jelly,

1½ oz soft brown sugar (not
  demerara),
powdered cinnamon,
2 heaped tablespoonsful soft
  white crumbs,
1 pint water.

Slice apples very thinly into roomy pan, add water, 1 tablespoonful powdered cinnamon and crumbs. Simmer until apples are collapsed, sieve, chill, add claret, stir well, add lemon juice, rind and sugar, stir again, stir in melted jelly add further generous pinch cinnamon. Pour into large jug. Refrigerate until moment of service. Add 2 ice cubes to each bowlful.

---

321 Soup au Vin Lyonnais

1 medium carrot,
1 white of medium leek,
1 medium turnip,
1 medium onion,
1 oz butter,
17½ fluid oz very ordinary
  burgundy,

25 fluid oz well-reduced beef
  bone stock (page 124) or
  chicken stock (page 125),
2 slightly rounded tablespoonsful
  fine tapioca.

Wash, peel and dice all vegetables. Dissolve butter in chosen pan, add diced vegetables, stir and shake over fairly brisk heat until they take up butter. Add wine and allow to reduce over a gentle flame until very slightly syrupy. Add boiling stock, then simmer with extreme gentleness with asbestos mat between pan and flame 1 hour. Scatter tapioca over surface, stir and simmer little more strongly for further 20 minutes.

322 Perlana Weinsuppe

18½ fluid oz well-reduced cleared
   beef bouillon or consommé,
9 fluid oz Perlana wine,
9 fluid oz cream or soured cream,

fried croûtons (page 17),
4 separated egg yolks,
cinnamon,
salt,
1 tablespoonful butter.

Place all ingredients except cinnamon and bread in wide-based pan over outer container of hot water. Whip steadily until piping hot. Add 1 fat pinch cinnamon, stir, pour into heated bowls, sprinkle again with cinnamon, hand croûtons separately.

323 Mosellesuppe (German Moselle wine soup)

3 eggs,
¼ pint water,
1 bottle Moselle,
sugar to taste,

2 rounded tablespoonsful potato
   flour or 3 rounded
   tablespoonsful arrowroot,
1 thickish slice lemon.

Separate yolks from whites. Empty wine into a wide-base pan. Stand pan in outer container of boiling water, set over low heat, allow to become piping hot. Meanwhile simmer water with lemon slice 5 minutes. Remove lemon, chill water. Use sufficient to transform chosen thickener to thin paste; add remainder to wine in pan. When wine mixture is hot, whip egg yolks into water/thickener, blend thoroughly. Pour on a little of wine mix. Stir, return all to pan and stir unceasingly to just below boiling. Add sugar to taste. Slip asbestos mat between outer pan and lowest possible heat. Spread stiffly-whipped egg whites over surface very carefully and evenly. Leave 20 mins. Ladle into soup bowls using wide ladle, pushing to pan-base each time to ensure foam makes fat dome on top of each serving. Serve immediately.

324 Biersuppe

1 pint light ale,
1½ pints strong beef bone stock,
1 flat teaspoonful of a mixture
   of cinnamon, nutmeg and
   mixed spices,
2 oz loaf sugar,

3 separated egg yolks,
3 tablespoonsful soured cream,
salt and pepper,
rounds cut from a narrow stick
   French bread.

Place beer, stock and sugar in roomy pan and stir until sugar dissolves over low heat. Place yolks, cream and one tablespoonful hot stock in small bowl and stir fast until creamily smooth. Return pan to lowish heat over asbestos mat to avoid curdling. Stir in cream mixture, add salt, pepper and spices. When just below boiling point serve in heated soup bowls adding 1 round of toasted bread to each base and pouring soup over.

Unclassified Recipes

325. Beef Tea
326. Barley Soup
327. Aigo Boulido
328. Kummelsuppe
329. Brotsuppe
330. Milk Soup
331. Mrs. Marshall's Remarkable Quick Cheese Soup
332. Mrs. Marshall's Cheese Soup
333. Stracciatella
334. Soupe Pour les Malades
335. Panade

325 Beef Tea

1 lb best possible, fat-free steak,   16 fluid oz cold water.

There are three ways this can be made to the best advantage.
1. Packed into a wine bottle, securely corked down, wrapped around with cloths which are tied securely and bottle set on a piece of wood in cold water in a securely lidded container.
2. Packed into (a) a Kilner Jar and stood on a piece of wood in lidded container; (b) a Fowler Lee bottling jar (our way) for those who have a steriliser.

The remaining procedure is constant. Lay steak on a wooden board and scrape meat into a pap with the sharpest possible knife. Pack (or stuff in the case of a bottle neck) into chosen container, add the water, secure lid. Leave for 1 hour to start "drawing out" juices. Then put into container surrounded by water and over very low heat. Allow water to come to what can best be described as "shivering stage" which is bubbling and boiling. Maintain like this for at least four hours. Then turn contents into a fine sieve and press *gently* with the back of a wooden spoon. When serving, warm but on no account boil. Just for safety tow a piece of absorbent kitchen paper over surface lest any particle of fat remain.

Yield approximately 12 fluid oz.

326 Barley Soup

4 oz pearl barley,
1 quart well-flavoured bone
  stock,
1 large coarse-grated carrot,
1 large coarse-grated turnip,

1 large coarse-grated onion,
1 bouquet garni,
salt and pepper,
1 tablespoonful concentrated
  tomato purée.

Place barley and bone stock with prepared vegetables and herbs in roomy pan, bring to boil, skim, steady off at simmer until barley and vegetables are tender. Season, remove bouquet garni, sieve or emulsify, return purée to pan, stir in tomato purée, re-heat and serve. Hand separate bowls of grated hard cheese and fried croûtons (page 17).

327 Aigo Boulido (Provençale Soup)

2¼ pints any well-reduced bone
   stock,
4 fluid oz olive oil,
½ flat teaspoonful salt,
2 peppercorns,

4 peeled crushed garlic cloves,
1 bay leaf,
1 rounded teaspoonful fresh or
   dried thyme,
salt and pepper.

Place all ingredients except thyme in pan with given stock. Boil, then simmer 15 minutes. Strip leaves from thyme or crumbled dried thyme. Stir in, pour into soup bowls, correct seasoning, optionally slide 1 lightly poached egg into each serving.

328 Kummelsuppe

1 rounded teaspoonful caraway
   seeds,
2 oz chicken fat (dissolved),
1 oz flour,

3 oz small-broken macaroni,
1½ pints strongly reduced
   bouillon (page 127),
salt and pepper.

Heat fat, stir in flour to soft-ball stage, add bouillon gradually beating well between each addition, stir in caraway, simmer 30 minutes. Meanwhile fling broken macaroni into plenty of fast boiling salted water, simmer for 10 minutes, strain, add to soup. Simmer soup for further 5 minutes, taste and correct seasoning.

Note: This soup may also be made with chicken stock (B page 125) after reducing stock strongly.

329 Brotsuppe

6 oz crusts,
1½ pints strongly reduced white
  bone stock,
2 eggs,
4 oz Austrian smoked sausage,

1 dessertspoonful freshly milled
  parsley heads,
salt and pepper,
1 scant flat teaspoonful castor
  sugar,
1 hard-boiled egg.

Dry crusts thoroughly by baking low down in oven. Break down into small pieces. Place in pan, pour half hot stock over, stand 10 minutes, emulsify, return to pan, add remaining stock and allow soup to reach boiling point. Meanwhile slice sausage thinly, then quarter. Do the same with hard-boiled egg. Whip up eggs, whip in 2 tablespoonsful soup, stir, return to pan, over hot water lest soup curdle, add sugar and heat without boiling. Correct seasoning, stir in sausage and egg. Sprinkle servings with fried parsley.

330 Milk Soup

1 quart milk,
2 egg yolks,
1 oz butter,
1 oz flour,

1 medium onion finely chopped,
1 fluid oz oil,
salt and pepper,
¼ pint single cream.

Skim wide-base pan with cold water. Put over low heat, allow to bubble, then pour in milk and allow to come to boiling point. Fry onion gently in butter and oil until very soft. Crush down with back of spoon, work in flour, dilute with a little hot milk, adding rest gradually. At service, beat egg yolks with cream, pour on a little soup, stir well, pour back but do not allow to boil again, taste, correct seasoning and serve Diablotins (page 12) separately.

331 Mrs. Marshall's Remarkable Quick Cheese Soup

1 oz flour,
2 oz finely grated cheese
  (Parmesan if possible),
1½ oz butter,
2 raw, separated egg yolks,
pinch salt,

generous pinch pepper,
1½ gills (7½ fluid oz) cold milk,
2 tablespoonsful stiffly-whipped
  cream,
10/12 fluid oz extra, hot milk.

You will need to use *only* the above ingredients, without deviation. You will also need to accept our guarantee that THIS WORKS, as it defies all the normal rules of sauce-making. Put flour, cheese, butter, egg yolks, salt, pepper and cold milk into a small, thick pan and stir very carefully over a moderate heat. As soon as butter melts and blends, add 2½ fluid oz milk gradually. Continue stirring, increasing speed to a wooden spoon beating until mixture becomes perfectly clear and very thick *as it will*. Now dilute with extra hot milk until desired soup-consistency is achieved. Remove from heat, beat in cream and serve with little fingers of hot buttered toast.

---

332 Mrs. Marshall's Cheese Soup

1 oz butter or chicken or pork fat,
1 blanched Cos lettuce, i.e. boiling water poured over then drained and dried,
5 oz peeled onions,
2 slim leeks both minced or finely chopped
1½ oz cooked chicken or other white meat, finely chopped,
1 oz flour,

3 pints well-reduced white stock,
¼ lb any melting cheese (best are Gruyère or Emmenthal),
2 oz grated hard cheese (best is Parmesan),
¼ pint boiling, single cream,
1 generous pinch nutmeg,
1 generous pinch pepper.

Soften chosen fat in frying pan, when "singing", turn in onions and leeks, set over low heat, cover and cook under lid with occasional shake/stir for 20 minutes. Shake flour over, stir/press until smoothly incoporated then dilute with 2/3 fluid oz given stock and beat well. Scrape into a saucepan. Stir in remaining stock, raise to gentle simmer and maintain 35/40 minutes. Five minutes before service, stir in meat, spices, shredded lettuce, cheeses and cream. Raise once again to boiling point—slowly—and serve with crusty bread, ideally a cottage loaf.

333 Stracciatella (Roman Soup with Egg and Cheese)

2 pints strong stock,
2 eggs,

2 oz grated Parmesan cheese,
1 tablespoonful fine semolina.

Heat 1½ pints stock, whip eggs with Parmesan and semolina, dilute with gradual additions of remaining cold stock, stir in a little of hot stock, when blended, stir into soup at just below boiling point, simmer 3 minutes and serve immediately. Remember—the egg flakes and is meant to!

334 Soupe pour les Malades

2 lb best lean steak,
1 unsalted pig's trotter,
1 empty champagne bottle and
  cork,

1 pan of water,
a little salt.

Shred beef raw, chop up trotter very small. Pack both into the champagne bottle and cork firmly. Wrap bottle in a tea towel and tie up securely being careful to cover base. Stand in pan of water and leave simmering for 8–10 hours. Strain off the small quantity of bouillon which you will now find contained in the champagne bottle, add a little salt (if permitted) and serve by the teaspoon, or leave to go cold and serve teaspoonfuls of resultant jelly.

335 Panade (Invalid Soup)

1 lb stale bread,
4 oz butter,
3 separated egg yolks,
salt and pepper,

extra milk,
¼ pint thick cream,
white bone stock (page 124).

Tear bread into small pieces (crust and crumb). Place in roomy pan with stock to cover liberally. Put over low heat, add butter in flakes, season lightly with salt and pepper. Simmer with extreme gentleness 1 hour 15 minutes, giving an occasional stir. Sieve, emulsify or liquidise. Blend egg yolks with given cream, remove soup from heat, stir in yolk mixture, beat thoroughly. Dilute to taste with extra milk. Heat through while stirring and without boiling. Correct seasoning.

Liquidised or Emulsified Soups

336. Celery and Cheese Soup
337. Clear Beetroot Soup
338. Jerusalem Artichoke Soup
339. Cooked Cabbage and Potato Soup
340. French or Runner Bean Purée
341. Winter Salad Soup
342. Apple and Onion Soup
343. Tomato and Courgette Soup
344. Goulasch Soup
345. Jugged Hare Soup
346. Oxtail Soup
347. Smoked Haddock Soup
348. Cottage Pie Soup
349. Gammon and Spinach Soup
350. Spring Vegetable Soup
351. Summer Vegetable Soup
352. Autumn Vegetable Soup
353. Mixed Iced Vegetable and Salad Soup
354. Iced Parsley Soup
355. Iced Spanish Vegetable Soup
356. Yoghurt Party Soup
357. Iced Cucumber Soup
358. Raw Mushroom Soup
359. American Iced Caesar Soup
360. Iced Johannesburg Soup
361. Iced Green Salad Soup (Winter)
362. Diabetic Vegetable Soup
363. Iced Green Salad Soup (Summer)
364. Iced Tomato Soup
365. Avocado and Yoghurt Iced Soup

336 Celery and Cheese Soup

1 small head celery,
2½ oz grated stale Cheddar,
salt and pepper,
1 pint clear bone stock,

1 pint milk,
1 flat eggspoonful celery salt,
1 small flat teaspoonful sage.

Wash, trim and chop celery. Place in a steamer over hot water and steam under lid 12 minutes. Place a quarter at a time into liquidiser, with ¼ of stock. Switch on full. When mixture is a smooth purée, empty into saucepan and repeat using all celery and stock. Stir in milk, salt and pepper to taste and finally celery salt and sage. Heat through and serve with fried croûtons. Hand extra grated, stale cheese in a separate bowl.

Note: Made with grated ends of over-dry Stilton this is particularly good.

337 Clear Beetroot Soup

cooked beetroot weighing 1 lb,
2 pints well-reduced strong bone
   stock,

salt and pepper,
1 smallest carton soured cream.

Peel and rough-cut beetroot and place in liquidiser in quarter quantities with same of stock. Switch on full. When pulped repeat with remainder of beetroot and stock, turn all into a saucepan, simmer gently for 15 minutes then strain. Heat through, taste, correct seasoning with salt and black pepper. Send to table in heated bowls with a blob of soured cream floating in the centre of each. When possible sprinkle fresh, freshly-milled parsley heads overall.

338 Jerusalem Artichoke Soup

1 lb peeled artichokes,
1½ pints milk,
¼ oz flour,
¼ oz butter,

2 rounded tablespoonsful grated
   stale cheese,
salt and pepper,
6 bacon rinds.

Bring milk to boil slowly with bacon rinds. Maintain at very gentle simmer 10 minutes. Steam artichokes until just tender, but do not allow them to collapse. Dissolve butter in a pan, stir in flour to form a roux, and cook for 3 minutes, stirring carefully to dispel all taste of flour. Add a little boiling milk from which rinds have been removed. Stir until smooth, add altogether sufficient milk to reduce roux to thin sauce. Liquidise steamed artichokes in small quantities with remaining milk. Blend resultant purée into the sauce, season with salt and black pepper. Re-heat as required.

339 Cooked Cabbage and Potato Soup

½ lb cold, cooked, old potatoes,
½ lb cold, cooked white cabbage,
1 raw, grated shallot or small
   onion,
salt and pepper,

1 heaped tablespoonful finely-
   scissored chives,
1 flat dessertspoonful freshly-
   milled parsley heads,
1 pint stock,
1 pint milk.

Rouch-chop both vegetables. Mix with shallot or onion. Liquidise in small quantities with small additions of given stock. Turn purée into saucepan, stir in milk, taste, correct seasoning and raise to boiling point when required. Stir in chives. Pour into heated soup bowls, sprinkle parsley over each serving.

340 French or Runner Bean Purée

1 lb cooked French or runner
   beans,
2 pints stock,
salt and pepper,

optional 2 tablespoonsful
   inexpensive dry white cooking
   wine or cider,
when available 3 torn basil
   leaves.

Mix beans, stock, basil and optional wine or cider in a roomy bowl, ladle gradually into liquidiser, switch on full, reduce to purée, and repeat, tipping purée each time into saucepan. Bring to the boil, taste, correct seasoning with salt and black pepper. Either serve immediately or re-heat when required. Little triangles of French Toast go very well with this and two may be floated, un-toasted side downwards on each bowlful.

341 Winter Salad Soup

¼ lb corn salad,
1 bunch watercress (both these well-picked and carefully washed),
½ pint tinned or bottled tomato juice,

1 pint stock,
the juice from 2 oz peeled onion grated coarsely,
salt and pepper,
1 flat eggspoonful celery salt,
½ a small rough-chopped garlic clove.

Mix all ingredients together. Ladle small quantities into liquidiser, switch on to half full speed and allow each addition to work down 30 seconds, then switch to full until all is in purée then empty into saucepan. Heat through and correct seasoning.

342 Apple and Onion Soup

½ lb (peeled weight) of eating apples, sliced fairly thinly,
1 large, chopped Spanish onion,

2 pints pork or bacon bone stock, well-reduced and cleared before using,
salt and pepper,
4 fresh torn or dried and crumbled sage leaves.

Mix all ingredients except seasonings together in a bowl. Ladle into liquidiser in small quantities, switch on full and leave each batch until reduced to purée. When all are assembled in saucepan, bring to boil over moderate heat, simmer 10 minutes, correct seasoning with salt and black pepper. Hand bowl of grated, hard cheese.

343 Tomato and Courgette Soup

½ lb courgettes,
½ lb thoroughly ripe tomatoes,
1¾ pints milk,
2 tablespoonsful thick cream,

1 two inch sprigs thyme,
4 fat stemless heads parsley,
salt and pepper.

Strip tiny leaves from thyme, chop and work into cream. Set aside. Wipe, top, tail, then steam courgettes until tender. Rough-chop and mix with skinned, rough-chopped, tomatoes, milk and roughly chopped parsley. Place in moderate quantities in liquidiser, switch on to full until all is in purée. Turn into saucepan, bring to boil, taste, correct seasoning with salt and black pepper. Pour into heated soup bowls. Drop blob of thyme cream into centre of each serving.

To serve as Iced Summer Soup, chill after boiling and seasoning. Ladle into cold soup bowls, add 2 ice cubes to each, five minutes before service. Place a spoonful of thyme cream in centre of each.

344 Goulasch Soup

When making a goulasch for a main course item, after cooking, set aside 2 ladlefuls of mixed meat and liquor and 2 heaped tablespoonsful of the cooked rice which accompanies this dish. Place these in a liquidiser with ¼ pint stock. Switch on full and reduce to purée. Turn into saucepan, add 1 flat dessertspoonful of paprika powder, a further 1 pint of well-reduced cleared stock and heat through. Ladle into heated soup bowls and drop a small blob of soured cream sprinkled with milled fresh parsley into centre of each bowl.

345 Jugged Hare Soup

When making jugged hare and just before serving, take out 3 oz of hare meat and 4 tablespoonsful of sauce, together with 2 small forcemeat balls. When making soup add to these ingredients, 2 tablespoonsful cooking-type port, 1 pint strong beef stock, 1 standard egg. Mix all together pell mell, ladle into liquidiser gradually, switch on full, empty purée into the top of double saucepan over hot water, ensuring egg will not curdle. Allow soup to heat through slowly. Then taste, adjust seasoning. Serve in heated bowls with 1 very small teaspoon of red currant jelly in each serving.

346 Oxtail Soup

When one or more oxtails have been cooked, take out 6 of the narrow little tail ends together with a cupful of the thick liquor. Let them cool and then remove the surplus fat. Refrigerate until required. Pull the meat from the bones, add to the liquor, emulsify with 2 sliced, steamed medium carrots and 1 medium sliced, steamed onion. Put all gradually in to liquidiser, switch on full and reduce to purée, dilute with strong beef stock to required consistency, taste and correct seasoning with salt and pepper.

347 Smoked Haddock Soup

When cooking smoked haddock in milk to be served with or without poached eggs on top allow an extra half pound to your main-meal requirements. When haddock has been poached until tender in shallow pan under complete covering of milk, some of which should be served with the fish course, set aside the additional 8 oz cooked haddock and whatever milk remains. Then when making this delicious fish soup, skin fish, flake it, place in liquidiser with 1 rough-chopped hard-boiled egg and up to 6 fluid oz of the salty, boiled milk. Switch on full and reduce to a paste. Place this in saucepan, stir in additional 1 pint fresh milk. Heat through, stir in a heaped tablespoonful of fresh or frozen parsley. Taste and correct seasoning, with probably only black pepper. Hand fried croûtons in separate bowl.

348 Cottage Pie Soup

Allow 6–7 oz of creamed potato and moistened mince mixture. Place in a liquidiser with 2 tablespoonsful of dry cider or dry white "plonk" wine, $\frac{1}{4}$ pint strongly-reduced beef bone stock, 1 generous pinch of dried tarragon. Switch on full and reduce to a cream. Turn into a saucepan, stir in further 1 pint strong beef-bone stock and bring to boil. Taste, correct seasoning, blend in 1 flat table-spoonful concentrated tomato purée and serve. Hand a small bowlful of grated hard cheese.

349 Gammon and Spinach Soup

This is a soup which should be made after the service of a gammon joint, when only 5 oz of meat remains from joint. Chop this up, fat and lean together. Remove stems from ½ lb well-washed spinach, then tear leaves up roughly. Place in liquidiser in two halves adding ¼ pint of pork-bone stock to each. Turn all into a saucepan. Add ½ pint milk, bring to the boil, simmer 5 minutes. taste and correct seasoning with salt and pepper. Add, and well-blend in 1 flat teaspoonful of made-up English mustard. Serve with bowlful of Pulled Bread, (page 12).

350 Spring Vegetable Soup

2 oz each of cold cooked carrots,
*   spinach, broccoli spears and*
*   potatoes totalling 8 oz,*
1 pint milk,

½ pint strong stock,
salt and pepper,
1 oz grated stale cheese.

Place all vegetables, cheese and ¼ pint milk in liquidiser, switch on full until purée is obtained. Blend into remaining milk and stock in saucepan. Bring to boil, taste, season with salt and black pepper. Serve in heated soup bowls.

351 Summer Vegetable Soup

2 oz each cold, cooked French
*   or runner beans, peas, chopped*
*   white of spring onion thinnings*
*   and raw, skinned, very ripe,*
*   tomatoes totalling 8 oz in all,*
salt and pepper,

generous pinch of chopped basil,
1 pint chicken-carcase stock,
¼ pint milk,
¼ pint top-of-milk or single
*   cream.*

Liquidise all vegetables, basil and top-of-milk at full speed until to purée. Turn into saucepan, blend in stock, then milk. Bring to boil, simmer extremely gently 5 minutes, taste, correct seasoning and serve.

352 Autumn Vegetable Soup

2 oz each of cooked, unskinned
  courgettes, aubergine flesh,
  shallots, and raw chopped
  mushroom stalks,
1 level dessertspoonful
  concentrated tomato purée,

1 fluid oz strained lemon juice,
1½ pints strong bone stock,
salt and pepper,
4 torn tarragon leaves,
1 fat pinch of powdered ginger
  and also of cinnamon.

Place all vegetables, herbs and spices in liquidiser with ¼ pint stock. Switch on full speed and maintain until all is in purée. Turn into saucepan, stir in remaining stock, bring to boiling point, simmer gently for 7 minutes, taste, correct seasoning, work in purée and lemon juice.

353 Mixed Iced Vegetable and Salad Soup

1 torn heart of cabbage or Cos
  lettuce,
1 oz raw, roughly-sliced white
  cabbage,
one 5 inch celery stick,
one 2 inch piece un-skinned
  cucumber, rough-chopped,
1 very small garlic clove,

1 skinned, ripe tomato,
½ a de-seeded, de-pithed green
  or red pepper rough-chopped,
1 sprig watercress,
pinch of salt,
strained juice of ½ lemon,
1 flat eggspoonful celery salt,
strained juice of 1 large orange.

Place all in liquidiser. Switch on to half full speed, maintain 1 minute, increase speed to full until purée results. Refrigerate until well-chilled. Stir in 6 ice cubes just before service.

354 Iced Parsley Soup

2 oz parsley (mixed stems and
  heads),
2 oz chopped celery,
1 oz de-stalked spinach leaves,
1 oz watercress (mixed stem
  and heads),

1 oz rough-grated young
  carrots,
salt and pepper,
1 flat eggspoonful each of celery
  salt and garlic salt,
4 fluid oz very strong stock.

Place parsley, spinach and stock in liquidiser. Switch on full and when in purée add watercress, whip down, then celery and whip down and finally carrots and all seasonings. Turn into jug. Refrigerate until well-chilled. Add 6 ice cubes just before service.

355 Iced Spanish Vegetable Soup

*1 medium, de-pipped and pithed
green or red pimento,
2 ripe, skinned tomatoes,
1 peeled, chopped garlic clove,
1 small rough-chopped shallot,
1 heaped tablespoonful
wholemeal breadcrumbs.*

*1 dessertspoonful olive oil,
1 teaspoonful wine or cider
vinegar,
salt and black pepper,
¼ pint strained tomato juice,
¼ pint chicken, veal or lamb
stock.*

Place stock, pimento and tomatoes with garlic in liquidiser. Turn on full and tip resultant purée into a jug. Then place all remaining ingredients except crumbs and seasonings in liquidiser and repeat. Blend both carefully, correct seasoning, stir in crumbs and refrigerate. Add 2 ice cubes to each bowl, 5 minutes before serving.

356 Yoghurt Party Soup

*2 cartons plain yoghurt,
4 fluid oz single cream,
2 oz diced, unskinned cucumber,
½ pint milk,
2 oz chopped, shelled shrimps,
1 chopped hard-boiled egg,*

*1 rounded tablespoonful each of
chives and parsley,
strained juice of ½ lemon,
salt and pepper,
4 chopped spring onions.*

Place prepared onions, 1 carton yoghurt, hard-boiled egg, parsley and lemon juice in liquidiser. Switch on full. When smooth and creamy turn into jug, stir in all remaining ingredients. Correct seasoning and add 6 ice cubes. Refrigerate until service.

357 Iced Cucumber Soup

*1 topped, tailed unpeeled
cucumber,
1 hard-boiled egg,
½ pint consommé
¼ pint single or coffee cream,*

*salt and pepper,
strained juice of ½ lemon,
1 carton plain yoghurt,
1 tablespoonful each of finely-
scissored chives and parsley.*

Slice cucumber into 4 strips lengthwise. Chop up roughly and place in liquidiser with rough-chopped egg, lemon juice and half consommé. Switch on to half speed. Maintain 30 seconds, increase speed to full and reduce contents to purée. Turn into jug. Stir in remaining consommé, whip in yoghurt, then cream and refrigerate with 4 ice cubes. Sprinkle chives and parsley over.

358 Raw Mushroom Soup

6 oz very fresh, unpeeled
  mushrooms with stalks,
1 pint milk,
1 raw egg yolk,

2 tablespoonsful onion juice,
powdered paprika,
salt and pepper,
optional garlic clove.

Place mushrooms in large sieve or colander. Scald with a kettle of boiling water. Rough-chop, place in liquidiser with optional peeled rough-chopped garlic clove, egg yolk, onion juice and 4 fluid oz of given milk. Switch on full, reduce contents to purée, pour into jug, taste, season with salt and black pepper. Add 5 ice cubes. Refrigerate until required. Pour into small bowls. Sprinkle powdered paprika fairly liberally over each serving.

359 American Iced Caesar Soup

1 small flat teaspoonful dry
  English mustard,
1½ oz of (ideally) Parmesan
  cheese,
4 well-wiped, rough-chopped
  anchovy fillets,
strained juice of 1 lemon,

2 tablespoonsful oil,
1 eggspoonful Worcestershire
  sauce,
1 torn heart of Cos lettuce,
6 fluid oz tomato juice,
1 pint cleared chicken stock,
salt and pepper.

Place all ingredients in a bowl. Stir and ladle gradually into liquidiser. With each addition, switch on full, maintain until all is in purée, then turn each succeeding batch into jug. Taste, correct seasoning with salt and black pepper, stir in 4 ice cubes, refrigerate until service. Pour into small bowls and hand fingers of piping hot grilled cheese on toast with this imperatively ice-cold soup.

360 Iced Johannesburg Soup

1 torn heart of Cos lettuce,
the skinless segments of 2
  oranges and 1 grapefruit,
1 small topped, tailed but
  unpeeled cucumber,
6 drops Tabasco sauce,
1 inch head mint,
salt and pepper,

1 gill (5 fluid oz) real
  mayonnaise,
1 carton plain yoghurt,
milk, optional, chopped garlic
  clove.

Place all ingredients except seasonings in roomy bowl, rough-cutting cucumber. Work up thoroughly, place small quantities in liquidiser. Switch on full, turn each batch of resultant purée into jug. Dilute with milk to desired consistency. Taste, correct seasoning with salt and black pepper, add 4 ice cubes and refrigerate until service. Pour into small bowls, and if liked, add a blob of whipped cream to centre of each and place half an orange and half a grapefruit segment upon each blob.

---

361 Iced Green Salad Soup (Winter)

1 chopped head chicory (endive),
1 small fat tip of mint,
1 small, carefully picked and
  washed bunch watercress
  with stalks,
2 oz rough-chopped celery or
  celeriac,

2 oz corn salad leaves,
1 rough-chopped garlic clove,
salt and pepper,
1 pint milk OR 1 pint strongly-
  reduced, cleared chicken,
  veal or lamb stock.

Mix all ingredients in bowl except half the chosen stock or milk and seasoning. Ladle small quantities into liquidiser, switch on, reduce to purée and turn into jug. When all is in purée stir in remainder of chosen fluid. Taste, correct seasoning, add 5 ice cubes and refrigerate. Pour into bowls and sprinkle with finely chopped mint.

---

362 Diabetic Vegetable Soup

1 breakfastcupful spinach,
1 small young turnip peeled and
  rough-chopped,
1 skinned tomato,
6 sorrel leaves (stalk-free),

1 small heart of lettuce,
2 pints clear veal or chicken
  stock,
a little thick cream.
All ingredients must be salt free.

Mix all ingredients except cream with half given stock. Ladle gradually into liquidiser, switch on each time to full speed and maintain until contents are creamy and smooth. Turn into jug. Stir, add 4 ice cubes and refrigerate. Add cream to each serving.

363 Iced Green Salad Soup (Summer)

1 torn heart of Cos lettuce,
6 young spinach leaves with
stalks removed,
2 well-sprouted turnip tops,
the stripped spikes from a
1 inch piece rosemary,
8 very slender sticks of sprew.
6 little trumpets nipped from
nasturtium flowers,
4 blanched dandelion leaves,

the grated zest of ½ lemon and
thin-skinned orange,
1 inch piece of skinned
cucumber,
salt and pepper to season,
½ pint strained tomato juice,
½ pint cleared stock,
1 de-rinded streaky bacon
rasher fried and then diced.

Place all ingredients except seasonings in a bowl and mix up thoroughly. Ladle small quantities into liquidiser. Switch on to full and reduce each batch to smooth cream. Turn all into a jug. Taste, correct seasoning, add 4 ice cubes and refrigerate until service.

364 Iced Tomato Soup

½ lb ripe, peeled tomatoes,
1 dessertspoonful chopped onion,
1 rough-chopped garlic clove,
1 tablespoonful wine or cider
vinegar,
1 faggot herbs,

4 peppercorns,
1 small blade mace,
2 heaped tablespoonsful very
fine soft brown breadcrumbs,
2½ fluid oz cooking-type sherry,
salt and pepper.

Place tomatoes in liquidiser with onion, garlic, wine or cider vinegar. Add 4 fluid oz cold water. Switch on full and turn contents when creamy into saucepan. Stir in 1 pint water, sink in herb faggot, add mace, allow to simmer over gentle heat for 30 minutes. Remove mace and faggot, stir in crumbs and sherry. Chill.

365 Avocado and Yoghurt Iced Soup

2 small peeled, stoned avocados,
2 cartons yoghurt,
1 carton soured cream,
1 small teacupful diced, skinned
cucumber,

4 oz shelled shrimps,
salt and pepper,
3 teaspoonsful strained lemon
juice,
strained juice of 2 oranges.

Place sliced avocado flesh in liquidiser with 1 yoghurt, the cucumber, lemon and orange juices. Switch on to half speed for 30 seconds, then increase to full speed until contents are creamed. Pour into jug. Add remainder and 2 ice cubes. Refrigerate.

INDEX

[Page Numbers]

217

218

219

220

223